The Ethics of Dissent

For the leaders and managers who insist on dissent,
discussion, and diverse thinking

The Ethics of Dissent

Managing Guerrilla Government

SECOND EDITION

Rosemary O'Leary

*Edwin O. Stene Distinguished Professor
of Public Administration*

University of Kansas

Los Angeles | London | New Delhi
Singapore | Washington DC

Los Angeles | London | New Delhi
Singapore | Washington DC

FOR INFORMATION:

CQ Press
An Imprint of SAGE Publications, Inc.
2455 Teller Road
Thousand Oaks, California 91320
E-mail: order@sagepub.com

SAGE Publications Ltd.
1 Oliver's Yard
55 City Road
London EC1Y 1SP
United Kingdom

SAGE Publications India Pvt. Ltd.
B 1/I 1 Mohan Cooperative Industrial Area
Mathura Road, New Delhi 110 044
India

SAGE Publications Asia-Pacific Pte. Ltd.
3 Church Street
#10-04 Samsung Hub
Singapore 049483

Acquisitions Editor: Charisse Kiino
Editorial Assistant: Davia Grant
Production Editor: Laura Barrett
Copy Editor: Judy Selhorst
Typesetter: C&M Digitals (P) Ltd.
Proofreader: Stefanie Storholt
Indexer: Teddy Diggs
Cover Designer: Rose Storey
Marketing Manager: Erica DeLuca

Printed in the United States of America

Library of Congress Cataloging-in-Publication Data

O'Leary, Rosemary, 1955-

The ethics of dissent : managing guerrilla government / Rosemary O'Leary, Edwin O. Stene Distinguished Professor of Public Administration. — Second edition.

pages cm.
Includes bibliographical references and index.

ISBN 978-1-4522-2631-6 (pbk. : alk. paper)

1. Dissenters—United States—History. 2. Administrative agencies—United States. 3. Whistle blowing—United States. 4. Business ethics—United States. 5. Retribution. 6. United States—Officials and employees. I. Title.

HN59.2.O32 2014
353.4'6—dc23   2013030670

This book is printed on acid-free paper.

16 17 18 19 10 9 8 7 6 5 4

Contents

Foreword

Edward Snowden was one of the thousands of analysts working deep inside the American intelligence community. He was a whiz at computer-driven analysis of top-secret information, including discovering patterns in the billions of email messages that fly around the internet. Since the September 11 terrorist attacks, the government's monitoring of that internet traffic had become an even more important source of intelligence. The terrorists, after all, had used the internet to plot their scheme and since then internet "chatter," as the analysts put it, became a gauge of the threats the nation faces. Snowden helped track the chatter as an analyst for the National Security Agency, an enormous super-secret organization at Ft. Meade between Washington and Baltimore.

Snowden didn't work at Ft. Meade or even in Maryland. Armed with a computer and an internet connection, he set up shop in Hawaii. And he didn't work directly for the federal government. He was an employee of Booz Allen Hamilton, one of the government's most important contractors. He held a top government security clearance but, ironically, it was a private contractor that conducted the background checks on this private contractor, who held some of the government's most important and sensitive secrets.

After working several years on the job, Snowden decided that the secrets he learned should no longer be secret. He leaked the inside story to the *Guardian*, a London newspaper, and launched an intense global debate over electronic snooping: by the federal government on its citizens, by the American government on foreign citizens and other governments, and by other governments as well. He became what Rosemary O'Leary calls a "guerrilla" and hopscotched the globe in a diplomatic cat-and-mouse game as he searched for asylum.

What turned an employee entrusted with government's deepest secrets into a guerrilla? He claimed that the more he learned about the government's activities, the more he concluded they were basic violations of civil rights. Indeed, much of what he disclosed shocked many Americans. But in the weeks that followed, despite intense investigations by reporters, there was no suggestion that the government's activities were illegal. Snowden simply concluded, on his own, that they were wrong.

As a condition of receiving his security clearance, Snowden had sworn an oath not to divulge those secrets. He decided to break that oath because he decided that disclosing the information to the world was more important than keeping his word. But that decision? that frames the very big and very fundamental issues that O'Leary explores in this important book. If an individual working for the government, even as a contractor, swears an oath to protect the security of what he comes to know on the job, is there any circumstance under which he can rightly disclose that information to others? Can a government worker choose to disobey orders on the basis of his own individual belief about what government policy should be? If all government employees are free to act solely on the basis of their individual beliefs, can there ever be enough coherence to government's activities to get anything done? And does it matter whether an employee works directly for the government or for a government contractor? Under what circumstances—if any—can and should a government employee go guerrilla?

Snowden's case attracted huge headlines, but as O'Leary's book makes clear, the puzzles of guerrilla government are widespread. They are raising increasingly important issues for government and how it works. The second edition of this wonderful book frames an exploration of these issues that is even more urgent.

Donald F. Kettl
University of Maryland
July 2013

Preface

This book is about guerrilla government. *Guerrilla government* is my term for the actions taken by career public servants who work against the wishes—either implicitly or explicitly communicated—of their superiors. Guerrilla government is a form of dissent carried out by those who are dissatisfied with the actions of public organizations, programs, or people but who typically choose strategically not to go public with their concerns in whole or in part. A few guerrillas end up outing themselves as whistle-blowers, but most do not.

Rather than acting openly, guerrillas often choose to remain "in the closet," moving clandestinely behind the scenes, salmon swimming upstream against the current of power. Their reasons for acting as guerrillas range from the altruistic ("doing the right thing") to the seemingly petty ("I was passed over for that promotion"). Taken as a whole, their acts are as awe inspiring as saving human lives out of a love of humanity and as trifling as slowing the issuance of a report out of spite or anger. Guerrillas run the spectrum from antiestablishment liberals to fundamentalist conservatives, from constructive contributors to deviant destroyers.

Guerrilla government is about the power of career bureaucrats, the tensions between career bureaucrats and political appointees, the intrinsic and extrinsic motivations of public employees, organization culture, the use of the media as a public management tool, collaborative public management, networked governance, and what it means to act responsibly, ethically, and with integrity as a public servant.

I have assigned the first edition of this book as required reading in several of my courses at the Maxwell School of Syracuse University, at the School of Public and Environmental Affairs at Indiana University, and at the School of Public Affairs at the University of Kansas. The courses in which the book has been used have included Public Management, Ethics, Public Administration and Democracy, Executive Leadership, Environmental Management, and the Role and Context of Public Administration. I have discussed this book with seasoned midcareer executives, graduate students, undergraduate students, and members of the general public from a dozen different countries. In every instance, the cases and the discussion questions prompted the most robust—and divided—debate that I have experienced in my twenty-five years in higher education. Specific questions that have emerged in these debates have included the following: If you are a government guerrilla, how do you *really* know when or if you are right? Where do you draw the line between sincere concern and arrogant hubris? When do the ends justify the means? At what point does guerrilla government violate professionalism? Is there, or could there be, a "dark side" to guerrilla government? How can a public servant dissent responsibly and ethically? Perhaps the toughest question to answer is this: How can a manager best manage guerrillas?

In anonymous course and lecture evaluations, participants have uniformly commented that this was one of their favorite readings, whether they agreed or disagreed with the actions of the public servants profiled here. When CQ Press sent the book to two sets of anonymous reviewers over the years, the comments were also uniformly positive. The reviewers loved the environmental cases but were curious about how guerrilla government activity played out in policy areas outside the environment. In response to these comments, I expanded the book to include additional mini–case studies of guerrilla government, which appear either as "interludes" between the larger cases or sprinkled throughout the introductory and concluding chapters.

This second edition contains many updates. A new chapter on Private Bradley Manning and the WikiLeaks scandal presents a riveting ethical dilemma that stands in sharp juxtaposition to the stories in the rest of the book. Up-to-date literature and theory supplement the first chapter. Epilogues enhance each of the three large environmental case studies to track what has happened in recent years. New ministories of guerrilla government improve the interlude sections. The analysis of the ethical challenges posed by guerrilla government in the last chapter has been revised to reflect the most current thinking. New questions for discussion are offered.

This book is organized as follows: In the prelude, I set the stage for the book and summarize its central thesis. In chapter 1, I provide a definition of guerrilla government and explain its connection with organization culture, with examples from a state environmental agency, NASA, the Pentagon, and the Office of the President. I also describe three lenses through which to view guerrilla government: *bureaucratic politics, organizations and management,* and *ethics.*

Chapter 2 is a case study of how guerrilla government took center stage in an attempt to save the wetlands in the state of Nevada. The story involves career public servants who attacked their agencies from the outside, marketed their cause by lobbying and fund-raising without the permission of their superiors, deliberately embarrassed the government, and managed collaborative networks.

Sandwiched between chapters 2 and 3 is the first interlude, which consists of four short descriptions of episodes of guerrilla government, one in the medical field, one in a national health insurance organization, one in radar support, and one in regulation promulgation.

Chapter 3 is a case study of guerrilla government in the U.S. Environmental Protection Agency's Seattle regional office during the era of Anne Gorsuch, the much-maligned and very controversial administrator of the EPA during the Reagan administration. The tensions between career public servants and short-term political appointees take center stage in this case study. The chapter highlights the management and policy-making styles of, and guerrilla responses to, three very different political appointees.

Between chapters 3 and 4 is the second interlude, with four more short stories of guerrilla government taken from the literature, this time in county planning, in the Legal Services Organization, in Job Corps, and in the U.S. Department of Labor.

Chapter 4 is a case study of how a government guerrilla sued his own agency—the U.S. Forest Service—to keep off-road vehicles out of the Hoosier National Forest. This episode emphasizes career public servants' clashing obligations to their agencies, the public, and themselves.

Between chapters 4 and 5 is the third interlude, with six more short stories of guerrilla government from sources as diverse as popular movies to casual anecdotes to handbooks for advocates. They concern the U.S. Central Intelligence Agency, the U.S. Department of Health and Human Services, a movement to protect schoolchildren from pests and pesticides, the U.S. Army, a state department of transportation, and the U.S. Environmental Protection Agency.

Chapter 5 is new for the second edition. It concerns Bradley Manning, the government guerrilla who leaked hundreds of classified government documents to WikiLeaks. Manning's actions have been called the largest security breach in the history of the world. This case brings into the spotlight the life-and-death aspects of guerrilla government and asks the reader to think about whether guerrillas such as Manning are heroes, villains, or something in between.

Chapter 6 summarizes the essence of the book. Here I look at guerrilla government as a whole and ask whether government guerrillas are ethical crusaders or insubordinate renegades. The chapter examines five harsh realities of managing government guerrillas and provides additional examples of instances of guerrilla government. It also presents the Association for Conflict Resolution's guidelines for managing conflict. Advice from the "pros" for managing dissent within organizations comes from a survey of members of the National Academy of Public Administration, alumni of the Maxwell School of Syracuse University, and some seasoned NASA officials.

A postlude asks, Are there lessons to be learned? Here I offer some new questions about guerrilla government designed to trigger reflective thinking. I have found these questions to be catalysts for thought among individuals with a wide array of backgrounds: those already in government service, those who aspire to government service, and those who merely want to reflect on the challenges of government service.

As this book goes to press, guerrillas in the U.S. Internal Revenue Service have been chastised for targeting certain conservative groups applying for tax-exempt status for closer scrutiny based on their names or political themes. In addition, Edward Snowden, a guerrilla government contractor in the U.S. National Security Agency, is hiding in Russia, fearing punishment for his act of releasing information about a secret government surveillance program involving telephone records. Guerrilla government is everywhere!

ACKNOWLEDGMENTS

In addition to the tremendous feedback from my students at the Maxwell School of Syracuse University, my students at Indiana University, and my students at the University of Kansas, this book benefited from comments provided by Don Kettl, dean of the School of Public Policy at the University of Maryland; Charisse Kiino, my editor at CQ Press; David Rosenbloom, Distinguished Professor at American University; Brian Polkinghorn, director of the Dispute Resolution Center at Salisbury University; Steven Maynard-Moody, professor at the University of Kansas; and my sister Kathleen O'Leary Morgan, a veteran federal and state public servant. Also helpful were my ace production editor, Laura Barrett, and my talented copy editor, Judy Selhorst. Six new reviewers provided insightful feedback based on their use of the first edition in their classrooms; their insights are greatly appreciated. They are Guy Adams, University of Missouri; Dennis Hatch, University of Wisconsin–Milwaukee; Kate Forhan University of Southern Maine; Alejandro Rodriguez, University of Texas at Arlington; William Wallis, California State University, Northridge; and Daniel Williams, Baruch College.

Also valuable were comments derived from my research presentations of some of the ideas in this book at Cornell University, the Chinese National School of Administration, the Chinese Executive Leadership Academy, the University of the Philippines, the University of North Carolina, Virginia Polytechnic University, Virginia Commonwealth University, SUNY College of Environmental Science and Forestry, Georgia State University, the University of Georgia, the Maxwell School of Syracuse University, Indiana University, and the University of Kansas; research presentations at the national conferences of the American Political Science Association, the American Society for Public Administration, and the Public Management Research Association; and numerous public lectures, including to the National Association of State Budgeting Officers, where members insisted that "guerrilla government happens all the time" in the world of public budgeting and finance. Funding from the Phanstiel Chair in Leadership and Strategic Management, the Hewlett Foundation, and the Indiana Conflict Resolution Institute helped free up my time to write. Finally, I am grateful to my husband, Larry Schroeder, and my daughter, Meghan, for whom "guerrilla government" has become a household word. Thank you for putting up with me.

About the Author

Rosemary O'Leary is the Edwin O. Stene Distinguished Professor at the School of Public Affairs and Administration at the University of Kansas, following a twenty-four-year career teaching at the Maxwell School of Syracuse University and the School of Public and Environmental Affairs at Indiana University–Bloomington. She is the author or editor of eleven books and more than one hundred articles and book chapters on public management. She has won ten national research awards and nine teaching awards. She is the only person to have won three National Association of Schools of Public Affairs and Administration awards, for Best Dissertation (1989), Excellence in Teaching (1996), and Distinguished Research (2004). An elected member of the National Academy of Public Administration, O'Leary was a senior Fulbright scholar in Malaysia and in the Philippines and an Axford Fellow in New Zealand. From 2003 to 2005 she was a member of NASA's Return to Flight Task Group, which was assembled in response to the *Columbia* space shuttle accident. She also has served as a consultant to the U.S. Department of the Interior, the U.S. Environmental Protection Agency, the Indiana Department of Environmental Management, the International City/County Management Association, the National Science Foundation, and the National Academy of Sciences.

Prelude

CHIUNE SUGIHARA was a government guerrilla. He was a Japanese diplomat living in Kaunas, Lithuania, with his wife and children during World War II. He was by all accounts an ordinary man; in fact a biographer could find nothing extraordinary about his background, skills, or personality (Levine 1996). In the summer of 1940, in direct disobedience of orders from his superiors in Japan as well as the Soviet government, he first clandestinely, and eventually openly, issued thousands of visas to Jewish refugees, allowing them to flee from the Nazis. His visas saved the lives of more than ten thousand Jews.

During his last month in Lithuania, Sugihara sat for more than fifteen hours a day writing and signing visas. By some estimates he did a month's worth of work each day. Any Jew who applied with any documentation whatsoever was given a visa without explanation. Sugihara did what he could to speed up the process in every possible way, even bringing in Jewish officials to help him with the processing of the documents. One author commented, "Sugihara . . . spent his foreign service in all sorts of clandestine activities. This came in handy. He knew how to operate outside the rules, yet he did not implement 'standard operation procedures' to prevent 'unauthorized use' of his stamps and seals" (Levine 1996, 5).

This routine continued for nearly a month. During that month, the Soviet government repeatedly insisted that Sugihara leave Kaunas. He ignored these orders and continued issuing visas. He also ignored orders from the Japanese foreign ministry to close and vacate the consulate. He continued issuing visas. He finally requested and received the Soviet embassy's permission to remain in Kaunas until the end of August 1940.

Sugihara continued issuing visas until the last minute, then burned all of his confidential documents to prevent the Soviets from confiscating them. He and his family stayed in a hotel before departing on a train. Sugihara posted a notice on the embassy gate telling people where he could be found. Many Jews came to the hotel, and Sugihara continued to issue visas from the hotel lobby. Later, as the train that would take him and his family safely out of the country started moving down the tracks, Sugihara signed documents with his arms stretched out the window of the train.

1

Sugihara eventually returned to Japan and lost his job in the foreign ministry, which caused him immense pain and embarrassment. He spent much of the rest of his life feeling humiliated. When asked why he did what he did in Lithuania, Sugihara responded, "I acted according to my sense of human justice, out of love for mankind" (Levine 1996, 282).

Fast-forward to June 2005. W. Mark Felt, also known as "Deep Throat," has outed himself as the ultimate American guerrilla. He is on the front page of every major newspaper around the world. He was the number two person in the Federal Bureau of Investigation during the Watergate years, and he systematically, clandestinely provided information about illegal actions of the Nixon administration to two *Washington Post* reporters and thus was instrumental in bringing down the president. (The pseudonym Deep Throat came from the title of an X-rated movie in the early 1970s.)

The Watergate scandal began with a burglary and attempted tapping of phones at the national headquarters of the Democratic Party in the Watergate office building in Washington, D.C., in 1972. Members of the Nixon administration were found to have engaged in covert spying on and retaliating against a long list of perceived enemies. President Nixon was directly linked to these activities when he tried to cover up his administration's involvement.

Felt went beyond merely corroborating facts: he proactively provided leads and outlined a conspiracy sanctioned by the president. In stuff that spy novels are made of, he developed a system of elaborate signals—from rearranged flowerpots on a balcony to drawings of the hands of a clock on newspapers—to communicate with a reporter that it was time to talk again. Most of his meetings with the reporter took place in a dark parking garage.

Carl Bernstein and Bob Woodward (1974), the two reporters who relied on Felt, described him as disgusted by the politics that

> had infiltrated every corner of government—a strong-arm takeover of the agencies by the Nixon White House. . . . He had once called it the "switchblade mentality"—and had referred to the willingness of the President's men to fight dirty and for keeps, regardless of what effect the slashing might have on the government and the nation. . . . Woodward sensed the resignation of a man whose fight had been worn out in too many battles. (130)

Others portrayed Felt as bitter from being passed over for the job as head of the FBI. Still others called him the conscience of the FBI. He "came to believe that he was fighting an all-out war for the soul of the bureau," wrote a family friend (O'Connor 2005, 131). Relatives described him as genuinely conflicted as to whether he saw himself as an American patriot or a turncoat. Mark Felt was an extreme government guerrilla, one whose "dissent" forever changed the way Americans think about the presidency.

As the second edition of this book goes to press, the latest high-profile government guerrilla is Private First Class Bradley Manning, who leaked hundreds of classified government documents to WikiLeaks. WikiLeaks publishes online submissions of secret information, information leaks, and classified media from anonymous sources and whistle-blowers. Manning's actions have been called the largest security breach in the history of the world. His story is told in Chapter 5.

Most cases of guerrilla government are less dramatic than the Chiune Sugihara, Mark Felt, and Bradley Manning cases. In fact, one of the central tenets of this book is that guerrilla government happens all the time in the everyday, often mundane world of bureaucracy. Sometimes guerrillas fail to correct superiors' mistakes and let them fall. Sometimes guerrillas fail to implement orders they think are unfair. At times guerrilla government manifests itself as the ghostwriting of letters and testimony for interest groups. At other times it may mean forging secret links with nongovernmental organizations. At still other times it may mean leaking information to the media. There are as many variations of guerrilla government as there are variations in guerrillas.

The central thesis of this book is that the majority of guerrilla government cases are manifestations of inevitable tensions between bureaucracy and democracy that will never go away. These tensions yield immense ethical and management challenges as well as several harsh realities. While all guerrilla government activity is not created equal, some guerrillas are canaries in the coal mine, telling us that something is awry. And while all guerrilla government is not heroic, some guerrillas just may become creative assets to public organizations if their dissent is listened to and channeled appropriately.

This can happen if such organizations strive to create internal cultures that accept, welcome, and encourage candid dialogue and debate. Public organizations need to cultivate questioning attitudes that encourage a diversity of views and encourage staff to challenge the organizations' assumptions and actions. It is essential for such organizations to improve their dispute system design processes so that multiple access points are offered and staff can easily identify multiple people as knowledgeable and trustworthy for approaching with advice about a conflict or the system. New political appointees must be educated about their own subordination to the rule of law, the constitutional requirements of their positions, the nature of legislative oversight, the desirability of working with career employees, and what it takes to lead in public agencies.

Chapter

1

Guerrilla What?

Guerrilla: One who engages in irregular warfare especially as a member of an independent unit.

—*Webster's Dictionary,* 2013

"Fire the bastard!"

My boss, the head of a large state environmental agency, was furious. I stood there speechless. He was a savvy, experienced administrator with a great track record. He had headed up some of the largest and most complex public organizations in the United States. He would eventually be profiled in the *New York Times* magazine.

"Fire the bastard!"

He was referring to one of my most creative, yet slightly eccentric, employees, Eric Jacobson. Jacobson tried to be a catalyst for change within our public agency. He performed a precise analysis concerning why our water quality regulations needed to be tightened and made more stringent, far exceeding federal guidelines. His ideas, while somewhat radical for their day, were not without merit.

The problem was that the bureaucracy wasn't listening. After hitting roadblock after roadblock within our organization, Jacobson turned into an independent environmental "guerrilla," working clandestinely with environmental groups who agreed with his notions about how wrongheaded our water policies were. He leaked information to the press and met behind our backs with elected officials. As he was a probationary employee, having worked for the agency less than six months (five months and twenty days, to be exact), legally we could still fire him "at will," my boss said, and we should. Someone had audiotaped Jacobson's presentation the night before at a public meeting where Jacobson had blasted my boss, our agency, and the governor for "caveman-era water policies" and slipped a copy of the tape to my boss. As he handed the tape to me, my boss yelled, "Who needs a troublemaking zealot like Jacobson around? Fire the bastard!"

In what proved to be a fatal career move for me (yet one I've never regretted), I went back into my boss's office the next day after listening to the tape and refused to fire Jacobson. "He is the leading edge of the system. He's creative and innovative," I argued. "He's a breath of fresh air. . . . We need people who are inspired and will challenge our thinking."

This time it was my boss who stood speechless.

"True," I went on, "he's a pain to deal with. True, I often go home and kick the refrigerator after meeting with Jacobson. But perhaps we can harness his resourceful insights for the good of the agency and the good of the public. I think we need to hear him out. I'm not going to fire him. If you want him fired, you'll have to do it yourself."

My boss never did fire Jacobson, but that exchange was the kiss of death for my relationship with my boss. From that day forward I received the cold shoulder from the person who once considered himself my mentor. He cut me out of many policy decisions even though policy was my primary portfolio. He made it quite clear that he was furious and insulted that I would question his judgment. Eventually I left.

For more than twenty-five years I have sought out others who have had experiences with what I now call "guerrilla government." Some were managers like me who sought to bring the Eric Jacobsons of the world into the fold, some were managers who "fired the bastards!" and some were guerrillas themselves. I even discovered a wonderful (now out-of-date) book titled *Guerrillas in the Bureaucracy* (Needleman and Needleman 1974) that concerns the impact of community planning programs. The authors use the term "administrative guerrilla" to refer to antiestablishment, advocacy community planners who often end up working undercover for specific clients rather than the nebulous public interest. Yet contrary to the authors' analysis, I've learned that there are no easy categorizations of guerrillas when government is examined as a whole, as guerrillas run the spectrum from antiestablishment liberals to fundamentalist conservatives, from constructive contributors to deviant destroyers.

The Government Accountability Project maintains a website (http://www .whistleblower.org) that provides hundreds of examples of whistle-blowers, famous and not so famous. In 2013, Cheryl D. Eckard, a former quality-control manager for Glaxo, a pharmaceuticals manufacturer, exposed the selling of "bad" drugs from a contaminated plant in Puerto Rico. In 2012, banker Kyle Lagow exposed the tax-evasion efforts of his former employer Swiss bank giant UBS AG. In 2011, Maria Garzino, a mechanical and civil engineer with the U.S. Army Corps of Engineers, publicly revealed the inadequacy of New Orleans floodwater pumps built by the corps after Hurricane Katrina. Then there are Herron Watkins, the famous Enron whistle-blower; Paul van Buitenen, who went public with claims of fraud and corruption within the European Commission; Bill Bush, the manager at the National Aeronautics and Space

Administration (NASA) who went public with the administration's policy of discouraging the promotion of employees older than fifty-four; and the unnamed U.S. Customs inspector who alerted Congress to security problems at the Miami airport after management took no action.

A few guerrillas end up outing themselves as whistle-blowers, but most do not. While they are unsatisfied with the actions of public organizations, sometimes even documenting fraud and abuse, they typically choose strategically not to go public in a big way. Their reasons for not going public are numerous and include fear of retaliation, as whistle-blowers often pay a heavy price for their actions.[1] Rather than fostering transparency, they choose to remain "in the closet," moving clandestinely behind the scenes, working against the wishes—either implicitly or explicitly communicated—of their superiors.

Guerrillas may cultivate allies among nongovernmental organizations (NGOs) within their policy areas, slip data to other agencies, and ghostwrite testimony for others. They may hold secret meetings to plot unified staff strategies, leak information to the press, and quietly sabotage the actions of their agencies. Their reasons for doing so are diverse—some are commendable, and some are disturbing. Most work on the assumption that taking actions outside their agencies provides them with a latitude that is not available to them in formal settings. Some want to see interest groups join, if not replace, formal government as the foci of power. Some are tired of hardball power politics and seek to replace it with collaboration and inclusivity. Others are implementing their own version of hardball politics. Most have a wider conceptualization of their work than that articulated by their agencies' formal and informal statements of mission, but some are more free-wheeling, doing what feels right to them. Many are committed to particular methodologies, techniques, or ideas. For some, guerrilla activity is a form of expressive behavior that allows them leverage on issues about which they feel deeply. For others, it is a way of carrying out extreme viewpoints about pressing public policy problems.

Guerrillas bring the credibility of the formal, bureaucratic, political system with them, as well as the credibility of their individual professions. They tend to be independent, multipolar, and sometimes radical. They often have strong views that their agencies' perspectives on public policy problems are at best not sufficient, and at worst illegal. They are not afraid to reach into new territory and often seek to drag the rest of the system with them to explore new possibilities.

At the same time, guerrillas run the risk of being unregulated themselves. Sometimes they fail to see the big picture, promoting policies that may not be compatible with the system as a whole. Sometimes they are so caught up in fulfilling their own expressive and instrumental purposes that they may not fulfill the purposes of their organizations. This is the dilemma of guerrilla government.

But given the possibility that guerrillas might be saying things that their organizations need to at least consider, why are these individuals often excluded by their agencies? Some agency managers, like my boss, see them as zealots, pursuing interests that are too extreme for government agencies that must serve the general public. More often, guerrillas are seen as championing values or interests that are in conflict with the status quo or unrealistic given scarce resources. Sometimes they work in agencies that are in denial about the need to change. Perhaps the organizations have poor communication systems, or perhaps the people who work there do not use the systems available to them. Sometimes guerrillas are involved in personality clashes or work in dysfunctional organizations. Other times they are embroiled in internal or external politics. Some guerrillas are a breath of fresh air; some are stubborn single-issue fanatics. There are multiple reasons why individuals go the guerrilla route and multiple reasons why their organizations might seek to exclude them.

I once worked with NASA on the Return to Flight Task Group (RTF TG) formed in response to the *Columbia* space shuttle accident. The *Columbia* Accident Investigation Board found that the agency's organization culture, which suppresses dissent, was 50 percent responsible for the accident (the other 50 percent had to do with technical engineering problems). Organization culture consists of the shared basic assumptions, values, and artifacts that are developed in an organization as management and staff learn from experience and cope with problems. The basic ways of thinking and doing that have worked well enough to be considered valid are taught to new members of the organization as the correct ways to perceive, think, act, and feel. Culture is for the group what character and personality are for the individual.

There are many stories about guerrilla government activities at NASA. For example, my RTF TG subcommittee was told that one of the codirectors of the Space Flight Leadership Council, a NASA insider, called a meeting of the council without notifying the other codirector, a retired U.S. Navy admiral and trusted friend of then NASA administrator Sean O'Keefe. The retired admiral had been brought in by O'Keefe in part to force cultural change in the agency. When the admiral's staff found out about the secret meeting, they notified the council that the admiral would be attending. The meeting was promptly canceled. That's guerrilla government.

When I discussed this issue with O'Keefe, his response was, "That happens everywhere." The more significant problem for NASA, according to O'Keefe, is far more subtle, yet far more pervasive: groupthink. Groupthink is an insular decision-making process in which the members of a group of decision makers are so wedded to the same set of assumptions and beliefs that they ignore, discount, or even ridicule information to the contrary (Janis 1972). Symptoms of groupthink include overestimations of the group's power and morality, closed-mindedness, and pressure toward uniformity.

At NASA, groups trained in particular disciplines routinely, perhaps subconsciously, dismiss the thinking of others trained differently. "The biggest battles at NASA are not between the agency and Congress as some might think," O'Keefe said. "They're between and among the diverse disciplinary groups, say the electrical engineers versus the aerospace engineers, or the biologists versus the astronomers, or the infrared light experts versus the comet specialists."

"It is not so much that dissenting opinions are crushed or shouted down, but they are automatically deemed improbable. The dismissing of other viewpoints happens so quickly and is so subtle that it is very tough to address as a leader," O'Keefe emphasized. A huge organizational challenge is how to maintain high analytic standards but nonetheless give due consideration to other perspectives that, if pursued, may reveal important new insights. Otherwise, as the former NASA administrator told me, "groupthink comes to accept deviations as long as they're within an 'acceptable' bounds without defining why something should be considered 'acceptable.'" In a life-or-death situation—such as a shuttle launch—such thinking can have tremendous impact on human lives.

At the individual level, organization members face an analogous challenge. They must guard against the human tendency toward believing that circumstances are tolerable, if not fully satisfactory, even when disconfirming information might be present. Thus one of the problems continually facing NASA is how to change the culture of the agency from one of groupthink, which could easily spawn more guerrilla government activities on the part of those whose ideas are quickly dismissed, to one that embraces a diversity of views and uses those differing viewpoints constructively.

A very different example has to do with a small group of extremists in the Pentagon who, in 2002–2003, manufactured fictitious scare stories about Iraq's weapons and ties to terrorists in order to bolster justification for the United States to go to war against that country. Many, including the U.S. Senate Intelligence Committee, which reviewed the decision to attack Saddam Hussein, concluded that these activities were in part fueled by groupthink. This is reminiscent of the case of Oliver North, who, under the Reagan administration, supervised the provision of covert military aid to the Contra rebels in Nicaragua in violation of the congressional Boland amendments, which prohibited the Defense Department, the Central Intelligence Agency, and any other government agency from providing aid to the Contras. My former colleague the late Senator Daniel Patrick Moynihan used to say that the implications of these actions for our constitutional government made his "blood boil." These are examples of a very different type of guerrilla government—one that allegedly operated with the approval of the respective presidents, but against the will of other superiors in the executive, judicial, and legislative branches of government.

Every seasoned public official with whom I have discussed guerrilla government has offered his or her own stories and examples of this phenomenon. For instance, I received the following e-mail message in response to my call for stories of guerrilla government:

> I worked for 35 years as a federal employee and now teach at American University. The instances of guerrilla government are far more widespread than you imagine. . . .

How do we make sense of this thing called guerrilla government? Are there any clues from the literature that might help us think more clearly about this phenomenon? The great thinkers in the social sciences have for years grappled with the concept of guerrilla government under varying labels and in diverse ways. Three major lenses, or vantage points, through which to view guerrilla government emerge from the social science literature; each offers a different type of understanding. These three lenses are bureaucratic politics, organizations and management, and ethics (see Figure 1.1). Below, I briefly introduce

Figure 1.1 Guerilla Government Lenses

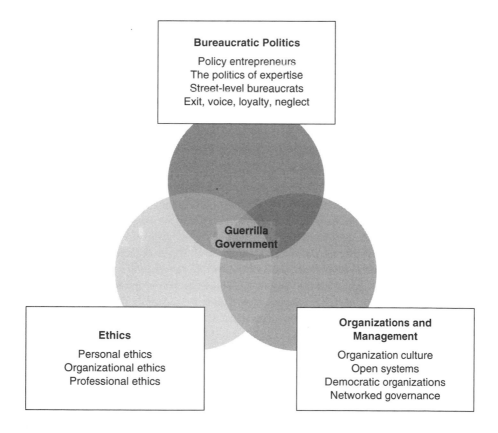

each of these to provide an analytical framework for understanding the stories that follow.

BUREAUCRATIC POLITICS

The bureaucratic politics lens is perhaps the clearest one through which to view guerrilla government. Paul Appleby and Norton Long are credited with launching this idea in the 1940s and 1950s in reaction to the idea of the politics-administration dichotomy that was so prevalent in the literature at that time. The politics-administration dichotomy was both a descriptive and prescriptive proposition that said that politics and administration are two totally separate endeavors and continued separation is the preferred arrangement. No, said Appleby and Long, this is wrong. Bureaucrats make policy through the exercise of discretion. This simple statement soon became embroidered with rich empirical studies and launched a long, deep, and rich ocean of literature on bureaucratic politics.[2] These classic studies of bureaucratic politics have yielded many relevant findings, listed in Box 1.1.

Box 1.1 The Classic Themes of the Bureaucratic Politics Literature

1. Bureaucrats make policy through the exercise of discretion (Appleby 1949).
2. Public administration is a political process (Appleby 1949; Stein 1952; Cleveland 1956; Key 1958).
3. Bureaucrats and bureaucracy are driven by their own highly particularized and parochial views, interests, and values (Long 1949).
4. Agencies and bureaucracies are constantly jockeying for power, position, and prestige, and this behavior has enormous consequences for public policy (Allison and Zelikow, 1999; Halperin, 2006).
5. Bureaucrats' views tend to be influenced by the unique cultures of their agencies (Halperin and Kanter 1973). In other words, where you stand (on a policy issued) depends on where you sit (Neustadt and May 1986).
6. All bureaucracies are endowed with certain resources: policy expertise, longevity and continuity, and responsibility for program implementation (Rourke 1984). Some bureaucrats are more successful than others, however, in using those resources to their advantage (Rourke 1984; Wildavsky 2000).
7. Policy made in an arena of bureaucratic politics is characterized by bargaining, accommodation, and compromise (Allison and Zelikow 1999). This is often a form of muddling-through incrementalism

influenced by nonrational factors known as bureaucratic politics (Lindblom 1959).

8. Agencies and bureaucrats within agencies will seek to co-opt outside groups as a means of averting threats (Selznick 2011).

9. Bureaucracies develop relationships with political institutions (such as the office of the president, governor, or mayor), and in the course of those relationships they give information, provide advice, make decisions, and administer programs in political ways (e.g., "Tell the president only what is necessary to persuade him") (Wildavsky 1986; Heclo 1978; Cronin 1980; Ripley and Franklin 1991).

10. Organizational arrangements within a bureaucracy are not neutral. They express an ordering of priorities and selective commitment undertaken with political motives (Seidman 1998).

Source: Adapted from Kozak 1988; Kettl 2011.

Several modern-day scholars have contributed to this lineage of thinking, including Meier, who has examined the bureaucratic politics of Hispanic education (Meier and Stewart 1991), family planning (Meier and McFarlane 1991), sin (Meier 1994), alcohol (Meier and Johnson 1990), insurance (Meier 1988), speed laws (Meier and Morgan 1982), and food (Meier 1978). Mashaw (1985) studied the Social Security Administration and found that career public servants successfully crafted their own version of bureaucratic justice comprising an internal law of administration. Brower and Abolafia (1997) carried out a series of ethnographic studies of political activities among lower-level public servants and found that those who engage in such activities use or create alternate channels because, from their vantage point, the regular channels are part of the problem. These lower-level participants gain identity and self-respect through their covert political activities as they struggle against the depersonalizing forces and irrationalities of bureaucracy. These works all give evidence in support of the idea that guerrilla government in varying degrees is a relatively commonplace activity that cannot be ignored.

Of great importance to the study at hand is the idea that bureaucratic politics involves strong political ties to clientele groups as public servants look to the groups they serve and interact with for security and support. Further, bureaucrats play politics as they interact with political institutions because policy is hammered out in issue networks composed of specialists from government organizations (see, e.g., Baumgartner and Jones 2009). These are just a few of the points made in the bureaucratic politics literature that are relevant to an examination of guerrilla government. The bureaucratic politics lens raises important questions concerning who controls our government organizations, the accountability of public servants, and the roles, responsibility, and responsiveness of bureaucrats in a democratic society.[3]

One subset of the bureaucratic politics literature is concerned with organization "deviants" (Ermann and Lundman 1978; Shaughnessy 1981; Punch 1984; Sims 2009). This literature also is relevant to the topic of guerrilla government, as much of it concerns "zealot" public servants (Downs 1993; Gailmard and Patty 2007), including whistle-blowers (Ting 2008),[4] and interorganizational protesters (Gummer 1986; Truelson 1985; De Maria 2008).

Two relevant literatures with different twists consist of writings on policy entrepreneurs and the politics of expertise. Policy entrepreneurs are "people who are willing to invest their resources in pushing their pet proposals or problems" (Kingdon 2010, 20; Mintrom and Norman 2009). Most of the examples in the literature of policy entrepreneurs are high-profile public figures, often called policy elites. Kingdon (2010), for example, discusses consumer advocate Ralph Nader and water-use reformer Senator Pete Domenici. Lewis (1980), in a similar vein, provides detailed case studies of Admiral Hyman Rickover of the U.S. Navy, J. Edgar Hoover of the FBI, and New York City parks commissioner Robert Moses, all policy entrepreneurs. Marmor (1990) analyzes the careers of Robert Ball and Wilbur Cohen, two giants in the history of social insurance in the United States.

Doig and Hargrove (1987) brought together thirteen scholars to write about thirteen high-profile entrepreneurs. Among those highlighted in the resulting volume are James Webb, administrator of NASA, who is often credited with putting a man on the moon; Gifford Pinchot, the first chief of the U.S. Forest Service; and Elmer Staats, comptroller general of the United States. The contributions to Doig and Hargrove's collection distill several of the conditions necessary for entrepreneurial leadership, including a governmental system characterized by fragmentation and overlap, public support for a particular policy area, a capacity to engage in a systematic rational analysis, an ability to see possibilities that others do not see, and a desire to make a difference.

Riccucci (1995) focuses on "execucrat" policy entrepreneurs—career public executives who made a difference. Still, Riccucci's policy entrepreneurs (for example, Edward Perkins, who helped break down the system of apartheid in South Africa, and Eileen Claussen, who negotiated and renegotiated the Montreal Protocol), like those just mentioned, all are at a much higher level in government than the majority of guerrillas. Roberts and King (1987, 1991, 1996) profile six policy entrepreneurs *outside* government who successfully introduced, translated, and helped implement new ideas into public practice, squeezing out lessons learned for those who seek to be change makers.

Brouwer and Biermann (2011) examine the approaches and techniques of policy entrepreneurs in Dutch water management and conclude that they use four types of strategies: (1) attention and support-seeking strategies to demonstrate the significance of problems and to convince a wide range of participants about their preferred policies, (2) linking strategies to connect their policies with other parties' projects and ideas, (3) relation management strategies, and (4) strategies aimed at influencing the times and places decisions would be made.

Guerrilla government is a mutant cross-pollination of policy entrepreneurship and the politics of expertise. The politics of expertise is a term used by Benveniste (1977), who examined why and how experts influence public and private policy. In an argument reminiscent of the one that knocked down the politics-administration dichotomy, Benveniste asserts that so-called neutral experts, primarily in the planning field, are in fact involved in politics, and "politics is never devoid of ideological content" (21). It is time to "shed the mask" of neutrality, Benveniste argues, and for professional public servants to admit that they are both experts and committed political actors.

Lewis (1988) phrases the same sentiment in a different way: "Among the many resources employed by public bureaucracies, professionalism and expertise are particularly significant. . . . When coupled with the ancient notion of the primacy of the state, they make for a formidable source of power" (158). He goes on to point out that with this expertise comes specialized knowledge, professional norms, and a prolonged attention span regarding issues that outlive the attention others in the political process can give. Hence professionalized public bureaucrats have a capacity to initiate and innovate that is unparalleled in the political system. They are truly political actors despite any label of neutrality they may give themselves or others may give them.

Kaufman, Hirschman, and Lipsky

Three great works spanning three different decades have tried to grapple intellectually with the dilemma of guerrilla government in three very different ways. Each merits special attention.

The first is Kaufman's *The Forest Ranger* (1960), which many consider the first of a series of important books taking an in-depth look at the importance of bureaucratic discretion. In that work, Kaufman examines the U.S. Forest Service of the 1950s from the ranger district upward. In his own words, the book is about how daily decisions and actions at lower echelons make concrete realities of the policy statements and declared objectives of the leadership. Forest rangers are members of the federal bureaucracy, yet much of their work is carried out in a decentralized fashion in locations far from Washington, D.C., in remotely dispersed locations. They have many masters: local residents, timber companies, ranchers, miners, conservationists, members of the general public, members of Congress, and the president. Despite the possibilities for fragmentation, the Forest Service of Kaufman's era was amazingly cohesive and uniform in action.

Much of Kaufman's book describes the mechanisms whereby the Forest Service leaders maintained uniformity and control of the diffuse organization, seeking in part to discourage guerrilla government before it could have a chance to germinate. As deviation threats increased, for example, central controls multiplied. As impulses toward fragmentation grew, the discretion of field officers was contracted. In order to narrow the rangers' latitude in decision making, the leaders saw to it that "preformed decisions" were made at all levels above the rangers (213). Rangers were thoroughly screened to promote homogeneity, while the Forest Service "manipulate[d] the intellects and wills" of its members (232). In-service indoctrination and training promoted standardization. An attempt to defuse differences of opinion was made prior to the promulgation of policies. Rangers' allegiances to local populations were neutralized through frequent rotation of rangers among Forest Service sites throughout the United States. The result was that the patterns of informal organization in the national forests were rarely at odds with the policies enunciated at higher levels, and centrifugal tendencies were vanquished. Forest rangers in the 1950s, in short, tended to "value the organization more than they value[d] getting their own way" (199). Is this the answer to guerrilla government? Alas, no. Despite these attempts to forge a tightly run Forest Service and the nearly all-obeying forest ranger, Kaufman acknowledges, there were exceptions. He notes, "In the last analysis all influences on administrative behavior are filtered through a screen of individual values, concepts, and images" (223).

A second work that merits special attention is Hirschman's *Exit, Voice, and Loyalty* (1970), an economic analysis of reactions to decline in firms, organizations, and nation-states. How can a book on the reactions to decline in firms, organizations, and nation-states inform the guerrilla government debate? Hirschman outlines a typology of responses to dissatisfaction: exit (leaving, quitting, or ending the relationship), voice (expressing one's dissatisfaction), and loyalty (faithfully waiting for conditions to improve). He is also concerned with the interrelationship of these options and asks, for example, if pursuing the voice option diminishes the possibility of the adoption of the loyalty option. Hirschman points out that these categories overlap at times, as when loyalists are especially vocal.

Farrell (1983) adds a fourth element to Hirschman's work: neglect. Neglect is defined as "passively allowing conditions to deteriorate through reduced interest or effort, chronic lateness or absences, using company time for personal business, or increased error rate" (Rusbult, Farrell, Rogers, and Mainous 1988, 601). While Hirschman's work was never intended to explain or predict responses of bureaucrats to dissatisfaction in public bureaucracies, it has been applied to such research by scholars such as Golden (1992, 2000), who examined bureaucratic responses to presidential control during the Reagan years in the Civil Rights Division of the Department of Justice and the National Highway Traffic Safety Administration. It has also been used in the marital counseling literature to explain the options of spouses who are unhappy in their marriages. While valuable, Hirschman's work does not begin to explain the complexities and intricacies involved in guerrilla government, but in Hirschman's defense, it was never intended to tackle such a broad range of subjects as those to which it has been applied.

Brehm and Gates (1997) go beyond Hirschman by defining the primary set of alternative actions from which a subordinate bureaucrat chooses, such as working, leisure-shirking (not working because one does not feel like it), dissent-shirking, and sabotage. Which option a particular bureaucrat chooses is likely to depend first on the bureaucrat's own functional preferences, second on the preferences of the bureaucrat's peers, and lastly on the efforts of the supervisor. Brehm and Gates found that strong functional and solitary preferences significantly encourage work and discourage sabotage. Caldwell and Canuto-Carranco's research (2010) furthers this finding by explaining why voice is the most effective moral choice for organization members dealing with dysfunctional leaders.

A third oft-cited book on policy making by career public servants is Lipsky's *Street-Level Bureaucracy* (2010), the first edition of which was published in 1980. While much of Lipsky's classic work does not pertain to the study at hand, some insights can be gleaned from it to illuminate the issue of guerrilla government. Lipsky analyzes the actions and roles of "frontline" public servants, such as police officers and social workers, and argues that they are essentially policy makers. This phenomenon is built upon two interrelated facets of these public servants' positions: a relatively high degree of discretion and relative autonomy from organizational authority. Lipsky helps us understand the "why" and "how" of guerrilla government: why guerrillas have so much power and how they might use it. While the guerrillas studied in this book are a mix of street-level bureaucrats, mid-level managers, and high-level managers (which Lipsky is careful to differentiate), they, too, tend to be in jobs with a great amount of discretion that gives them a certain amount of power. So, too, do the guerrillas studied here enjoy relative autonomy—up to a point—from organizational authority.

Vinzant and Crothers (1998) examine successful street-level bureaucrats and find in them many of the leadership skills enunciated earlier in Doig and Hargrove's collection of analyses of agency heads. Maynard-Moody and Musheno (2003) take Lipsky's analysis one step further by offering multiple stories told by "the coal miners of policy" (157). These stories highlight the fact that frontline workers' beliefs and values are formed in "rough-and-tumble interaction with peers and citizen-clients, not in regulated, formal interaction with supervisors" (157). Frontline workers' actions demonstrate the immense freedom that lower-level public servants have to use their own discretion, as well as the fact that much of the organization culture that informs those actions comes from stories passed on from one worker to the next.

The empirical literature of the past ten years adds to these perspectives. Riccucci (2005) studied street-level bureaucrats implementing policies for the Temporary Assistance for Needy Families program in Michigan and found that their discretionary decisions were affected more by clients than by supervisors. DeHart-Davis (2007) analyzed the "unbureaucratic personality" and found, seemingly paradoxically, a negative correlation between an individual's public service commitment and that individual's willingness to bend rules, as guerrillas often do. Oberfield (2010) investigated rule following and discretion at the front lines of government and found that the bureaucrats' views of rule following remained largely unchanged from the views they held when they entered the organization. Oberfield (2012) then studied how police officers develop their views about using force and concluded that self-selection (personality) and socialization while on the job combine to influence those views. Tummers and Van de Walle (2012) scrutinized health care professionals' resistance to change and found that it was largely driven by professional belief that the change would not serve clients or save money, followed by personal self-interest, including a fear of loss of status, income, and administrative discretion.

Thus the reality of bureaucratic politics is both good and bad. At best, bureaucratic politics allows career public servants the discretion to make sense out of their day-to-day challenges, to act in ways that they deem fair, just, and equitable. At worst, bureaucratic politics is a form of arrogance that allows public servants to act according to their own whims, perhaps to stereotype, and to invent ways of dealing with public policy challenges that may or may not comport with the will of people.

ORGANIZATIONS AND MANAGEMENT

Equally as important as the concept of organization culture is the concept of the environment of organizations. The classic organization theorists, such as Cyert and March (1992), Emery and Trist (1965), Katz and Kahn (1978), Thompson (1967), Lawrence and Lorsch (1969), and Aldrich (1972), all maintain that organizations both are shaped by and seek to shape the environments in which they exist. This "open systems" approach to understanding organizations maintains that organizations are in constant interaction with their environments, that organization boundaries are permeable, and that organizations both consume resources and export resources to the outside world. In other words, organizations do not exist in a vacuum.

This notion contrasts with traditional theories that tended to view organizations as "closed systems," which led to an overemphasis on the internal functioning of organizations. While the internal functioning of an organization is significant and cannot be ignored, it is essential to remember that all organizations "swim" in tumultuous environments that affect every organizational level. The open systems perspective is important to any analysis of public organizations and especially to thinking about guerrilla government. Public organizations, such as those profiled in this book, seek to thrive in environments that include influences by the concerned public, elected officials, the judiciary, interest groups, and nongovernmental organizations, to name just a few significant entities. Working with, and being influenced by, individuals and groups outside their own organizations has long been a fact of life for public servants (Gaus 1947; Brownlow 1959; Wildavsky 2004; Stillman 2004). In addition, these individuals exist in social networks—both inside and outside their organizations—that influence their ideas, attitudes, and behaviors (Moynihan and Pandey 2008).

Perhaps the most exciting modern offshoot of the open systems perspective is that of networked governance. A network is a spiderweb of relationships and connections between and among individuals, organizations, and jurisdictions dedicated to a common purpose. Every guerrilla profiled in this book is part of, and used to his or her advantage, an extensive network. O'Toole (1997) describes networks as a

> pattern of two or more units, in which not all the major components are encompassed within a single hierarchical array. . . . Networks are structures of interdependence involving multiple organizations or parts thereof. . . . The institutional glue congealing networked ties may include authority bonds, exchange relations, and coalitions based on common interest. (45)

O'Toole contrasts the reality of networks with the dominant picture portrayed in courses, texts, and standard theories, that of a universe centered on the individual agency and its management.

Among the first public management scholars to develop a theory of networked governance were Provan and Milward (1995), who studied the implementation of mental health programs in four cities and established the importance of network linkages between and among organizations and individuals. LaPorte (1996) points out that trust becomes increasingly vital in networked arrangements because of the importance of collaboration. In reality, managers in networked settings do not supervise most of those on whom their own success depends (O'Toole 1997). Since administrators do not necessarily possess authority, they may actually weaken their own influence by giving directives. Facilitation, negotiation, conflict management, and collaborative problem-solving skills become extremely important (O'Leary and Bingham, 2007; O'Leary and Vij 2012), as do individual attributes such as having an open mind, being trustworthy, and being self-aware (O'Leary, Choi, and Gerard 2012; O'Leary and Gerard 2012, 2013).

A growing literature on "collaborative public management" (Kettl 2002; Agranoff and McGuire 2004) analyzes the boundary-spanning activities of public servants who are trying to solve problems that cannot be solved easily by a single organization (see also O'Leary and Bingham 2009; Bingham and O'Leary 2008). Public servants find themselves seeking ways to shift network membership toward more supportive coalitions, locating key allies, and attempting to build collaborations of organizations and people. The collaborative public management literature can help us understand the reality of the spiderwebs of acquaintances and partnerships in which the guerrillas studied in this book thrived.

ETHICS

Ethics is the study of values and how to define right and wrong action (Van Wart 1996; Menzel 1999; Cooper 2001, 2012). Ethics is more than just thinking about right and wrong—it is doing right, not wrong. As those who study ethics like to say, ethics is not a spectator sport—it is a contact sport. Therefore, the ethical lens is, in my view, the most important lens through which to view guerrilla government, yet it is perhaps also the most difficult to think about in a concrete fashion. What constitutes ethical behavior and how do we ensure it? Who decides what is ethical and what is not?

Waldo (1988) offers a map of the ethical obligations of public servants, with special reference to the United States, that is especially applicable to the issue of guerrilla government. In his map, presented here in Figure 1.2, Waldo identifies a

Figure 1.2 Waldo's Map: Ethical Obligations of a Public Servant

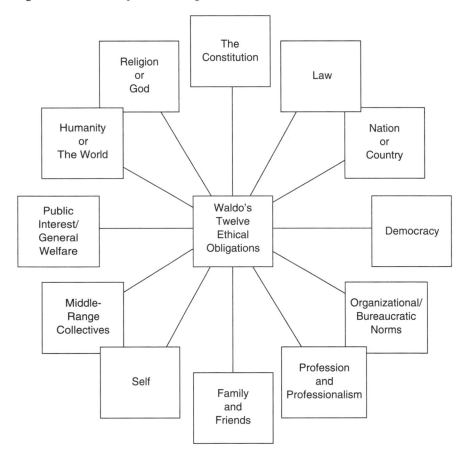

dozen sources and types of ethical obligations, but he cautions that the list is capable of "indefinite expansion" (103) and that the obligations do not lend themselves to any prioritization.

The first ethical obligation is an *obligation to the Constitution.* The upholding of regime and regime values, Waldo writes, is a typical source of public servant obligations. In the United States the Constitution is the foundation of regime and regime values (Richardson 1997). This sentiment is in sync with that expressed by Rohr (1986), who maintains that nothing is more fundamental to governance than a constitution. It also comports with the opinion of Rosenbloom, Carroll, and Carroll (2000), who maintain that "constitutional competence" is essential for all public managers.

A second obligation of public servants is an *obligation to law.* This refers to the laws made pursuant to, and in addition to, the Constitution. Public servants must follow and implement the law. But, Waldo asks, what if the law is unclear? What if laws conflict?

Next Waldo tackles a public manager's *obligation to nation or country.* Waldo points out that in many situations obligation to one's "Fatherland, Motherland, Homeland" (104) overrides the obligation to regime. President Abraham Lincoln articulated this tension in a letter dated April 4, 1864, when, in justifying his actions to end slavery, he asked, "Was it possible to lose the Nation, and yet preserve the Constitution?"

Obligation to democracy is next on Waldo's map for public servants. Waldo explains democracy as the will of the people, but then asks several provocative questions: How do we know the will of the people? It is intertwined with the Constitution, but it is not 100 percent contained in the Constitution. What about other laws? What about avenues in addition to law? And is the will of the people to be put ahead of the welfare of the people, say, when a public servant has information not available to the people? Ethicist Louis C. Gawthrop (1998) takes this obligation one step further:

> To labor in the service of democracy is to recognize that all of us are called, in one way or another, in varying degrees of responsibility, to be watchmen, sentinels, or prophets for others—any others—as well as for one another, in attempting to attain the common good. . . . public administrators must be willing to confront the suppressive and debilitating constraints that are currently being imposed on "bureaucracy" from all directions, and to reaffirm the values and virtues inherent in the notion of service that have unified the ethical forces of democracy in the past. Public service in the spirit of democracy demands an unqualified commitment to the common good. Nothing less will do; nothing more is needed. (100–101)

Obligation to organizational/bureaucratic norms is another competing obligation with which public servants must grapple. Such obligations are both generic and specific. Generic obligations can be found in most, if not all, public bureaucracies in the United States: loyalty, duty, order, economy, efficiency. Specific organizational/ bureaucratic norms will change from organization to organization depending on the function of the organization, the clientele, and the technology. The Forest Service, as profiled in Kaufman's book, is a good example of an organization with strong bureaucratic norms.

A sixth obligation espoused by Waldo is *obligation to profession and professionalism*. Most professions have established tenets that act to shape the values and behavior of their members. Most professions also have codes of ethics that members must follow. The American Society for Public Administration's code of ethics states that public servants should serve the public interest, respect the Constitution and the law, demonstrate personal integrity, promote ethical organizations, and strive for professional excellence (see Box 1.2). It is interesting to note that up until March 2013, the ASPA code of ethics included a clause that stated that respecting the Constitution and the law includes "encouraging and facilitating legitimate dissent activities."

Box 1.2 Code of Ethics of the American Society for Public Administration

---

The American Society for Public Administration (ASPA) advances the science, art, and practice of public administration. The Society affirms its responsibility to develop the spirit of responsible professionalism within its membership and to increase awareness and commitment to ethical principles and standards among all those who work in public service in all sectors. To this end, we, the members of the Society, commit ourselves to uphold the following principles:

1. *Advance the public interest.* Promote the interests of the public and put service to the public above service to oneself.
2. *Uphold the Constitution and the law.* Respect and support government constitutions and laws, while seeking to improve laws and policies to promote the public good.
3. *Promote democratic participation.* Inform the public and encourage active engagement in governance. Be open, transparent, and responsive, and respect and assist all persons in their dealings with public organizations.
4. *Strengthen social equity.* Treat all persons with fairness, justice, and equality and respect individual differences, rights, and freedoms. Promote affirmative action and other initiatives to reduce unfairness, injustice, and inequality in society.
5. *Fully inform and advise.* Provide accurate, honest, comprehensive, and timely information and advice to elected and appointed officials and governing board members, and to staff members in your organization.

6. *Demonstrate personal integrity.* Adhere to the highest standards of conduct to inspire public confidence and trust in public service.
7. *Promote ethical organizations.* Strive to attain the highest standards of ethics, stewardship, and public service in organizations that serve the public.
8. *Advance professional excellence.* Strengthen personal capabilities to act competently and ethically and encourage the professional development of others.

Next on Waldo's map is *obligation to family and friends.* In the United States we generally have an ethos that obligation to family and friends cannot or should not supersede other ethical obligations of public servants. Yet in many other countries in which family or other social group remains the center of loyalty and values, Waldo points out, public servants choose family and friends over their other ethical obligations, making the creation of an effective government impossible.

Waldo's eighth obligation is *obligation to self.* As Shakespeare says, "To thine own self be true." At the end of a long day, can you look at yourself in the mirror and feel good about what you've done? "The argument for *self,*" Waldo writes, "is that self-regard is the basis for other-regard, that proper conduct toward others, doing one's duty, must be based on personal strength and integrity" (105).

Obligation to middle-range collectives is next on Waldo's map. Examples include obligations to political party, class, ethnic group, gender, union, church, and interest group, to mention just a few possibilities. These can, and do, pose ethical obligations to public servants.

Obligation to the public interest or the general welfare is one that is often articulated by public servants and is often espoused in the literature. Waldo points out that this obligation has linkages to many of the other obligations: to the Constitution, to nation, and to democracy, for example. It is one of the most difficult concepts to operationalize, yet one of the powerful pulls a public servant may feel.

Waldo's eleventh duty is *obligation to humanity or the world.* Waldo sums it up best:

> It is an old idea, and perhaps despite all a growing idea, that an obligation is owed to humanity in general, to the world as a total entity, to the future as the symbol and summation of all that can be hoped. All "higher" religions trend in this direction, however vaguely and imperfectly. It is certainly an ingredient in various forms of one-world consciousness, and it figures prominently in the environmental ethic and in ecological politics. (106)

Waldo ends his map with an *obligation to religion or to God.* For many individuals religion and God are one and the same, but for others the two are separate and distinct. This obligation can pose formidable challenges for those public servants who view it as clashing with their other obligations, such as to the law or to organizational/ bureaucratic norms. A missionary acquaintance of mine wears a necklace with a pendant that reads in Greek, "God is first, family and friends are second, and I am third." This expresses his personal hierarchy of competing obligations.

Other important perspectives through which to view guerrilla government abound in the literature. A few stand out. For example, Cooper (2012, 65–89), citing Mosher (1968), maintains that responsibility is the key to ethical behavior in the public sector. This includes objective responsibility (e.g., what the law says) and subjective responsibility (e.g., personal and professional beliefs). Cooper urges public managers facing ethical dilemmas to identify all possible alternatives, project probable consequences, and analyze those consequences by viewing them through the lenses of moral rules and ethical principles, by conducting self-appraisal, and by thinking through how they might defend their actions before a broad audience.

The more recent literature challenges us to think more deeply about the connection between bureaucratic discretion and ethical dilemmas. O'Kelly and Dubnick (2006) maintain that issues of administrative discretion can be thought of more seriously as moral challenges. Bruhn (2009) argues that all organizations have gray areas where the line between right and wrong is blurred, but major decisions are made nonetheless, catalyzing ethical challenges. Echoing this sentiment are Loyens and Maesschalck (2010), who argue that there is common ground between ethical dilemmas and discretion in policy implementation. Heintzman (2007) and Getha-Taylor (2009) separately argue that in order to reestablish public trust, government must make ethical behavior a priority, and this requires attention to public service values.

The implications of guerrilla government for democracy are a very critical concern. As you read about the episodes of guerrilla government that follow, ask yourself which of these competing obligations each of the guerrillas was responding to. What is each guerrilla's obligation hierarchy? What should it be? Even though the work they do may arguably be commendable, are guerrillas going against the state? Are they subverting the mandates of elected officials? Are they following the letter of the law but breaking the spirit of the law? What makes their ideals "right" and "just" for the people? Are they "doing the right thing"?

LOOKING AHEAD

While each of the authors whose work is highlighted above offers unique and valuable insights, taken as a whole these scholars pose more questions than they answer, inviting a closer examination of the guerrilla government phenomenon. I wanted to know more about these so-called guerrillas, such as who they are and why they developed counteragency agendas. I wanted to know to what extent organizational systems account for multiple causes of guerrilla government. I wanted to know whether there are models of organizational systems that allow a voice for these individuals. I wanted to know whether it is possible to keep guerrillas in, or bring them back into, the affairs of an organization. I wanted to know whether there is a link between the formal and informal procedures for resolving conflict within agencies and the prevalence of guerrilla government. These are some of the questions addressed in this book.

As I was concluding my work on the first edition of this book, my phone rang. It was a biologist friend from Arizona. She knew about the book I was writing, and she wanted to know if I had heard about Dave Wegner, a scientist and government guerrilla at the Bureau of Reclamation (BOR) within the U.S. Department of the Interior (DOI) who successfully waged an "environmental war" in the Grand Canyon. Wegner, she told me, was instrumental in coordinating the first-ever Grand Canyon spike release (the rapid release of large quantities of water) to simulate natural conditions of water flow through the canyon. He appeared on television with Bruce Babbitt, then secretary of the interior, achieving hero status among many scientists, conservationists, and environmentalists. Wegner eventually publicly blasted Babbitt when they disagreed on future policy and later lost his BOR job. His job officially was phased out and his office moved to Denver, but knowledgeable insiders say that the truth is that those in charge got tired of Wegner's behind-the-scenes guerrilla activities to promote his pet cause.

I flew to Washington, D.C., to interview Daniel Beard, former commissioner of the Bureau of Reclamation and then president of the Audubon Society, who called himself Dave Wegner's "protector." He told me that Wegner was not "one of the Bureau boys." Wegner's guerrilla government way of operating was controversial within the BOR. As director of the Grand Canyon Environmental Studies Office (GCESO), Wegner forged linkages with members of the local, state, national, and international scientific community by parceling out grants for the study of the Grand Canyon ecosystem. The grant funds came from the hydropower industry, which gave money annually to the GCESO "in order to look good and to get the environmentalists off their backs," Beard told me. The fact that the funds were not kept in-house, and that Wegner was able to forge a huge network of supporters by leveraging these funds, was a source of irritation to many inside the BOR.

Wegner initiated a National Academy of Sciences (NAS) study to bring good science to policy decisions concerning the Grand Canyon. Yet he used the NAS for both scientific and political purposes. The NAS panel provided invaluable feedback about the scientific studies being done and not being done in the Grand Canyon. At the same time, when the NAS gave Wegner the stamp of approval, he used it to fend off his opponents and naysayers.

Wegner participated in fund-raisers to save the Grand Canyon and the Colorado River, helped draft legislation aimed at protecting both, was an instrumental force behind the scenes in the making of several documentary films about the environmental problems there, and was a master at cultivating positive relations with the media. It was not unusual for Wegner to plan and implement extravagant media blitzes either directly with the press or through leaks to environmental and scientific organizations.

Other Wegner links with environmental groups were well-known: he would ghostwrite letters and testimony to be delivered to elected officials, and he had a hand in every major environmental bill introduced concerning the Grand Canyon in a twenty-year period. He was a master at lobbying, fund-raising, and cultivating congressional staff as allies. There was also a passive-aggressive side to Wegner, Beard told me. He would often not implement orders he thought were unfair, unwise, or possibly harmful to the ecosystem of the Grand Canyon. He was not a bureau man, but a Grand Canyon man. His allegiance clearly was not to the DOI, but to the environment. It was also not unusual for Wegner to hold clandestine meetings to plot a unified strategy among staff and nonstaff scientists if he was convinced that such actions were needed to protect the environment.

With another great guerrilla episode halfway written, I flew out to Arizona to interview Dave Wegner himself. After a four-hour discussion that was closer to an interrogation, I realized that he was resisting telling me his story. He would neither confirm nor deny what my biologist friend and Beard had told me. He did not want to talk. A chapter in my book about his actions could make his life miserable, he finally said. He abruptly ended the interview. I had hit a dead end.

Similarly, after writing up a different chapter on guerrilla government activities, this time concerning housing policy in a major metropolitan area, I e-mailed it to the guerrilla and asked if I had portrayed the facts correctly. I received the following response from him:

Dear Professor O'Leary,

Thank you for forwarding your write-up of my story to me. To answer your question, yes you have portrayed the facts of my case 100% correctly. However, regretfully, I am not giving you permission to use my story as I am too easily identifiable from the details of the situation to colleagues here. . . . I plan to retire next summer after which my anxiety over publication would be significantly lessened, but right now I don't wish to unnecessarily complicate my final year of state service.

While I have hit many similar brick walls over the years, I fortunately also have interviewed dozens of guerrillas who were willing to share their stories with me. Chapters 2, 3, and 4 offer in-depth stories of guerrilla government that started with such interviews, and chapter 5 offers a new story concerning the WikiLeaks scandal, although my requests to interview Private Bradley Manning regrettably were denied by officials at the U.S. Penitentiary Leavenworth. I selected the stories related in chapters 2, 3, and 4 from among many told to me over the past twenty-five years because, first, the guerrillas themselves agreed to provide information; second, they were verifiable by multiple sources; and third, they provide clear examples of an array of guerrillas, why they did what they did, and the roles their organizations played in catalyzing their guerrilla activities. Chapter 5 details the amazing story, covered broadly in the international media, of a government guerrilla who leaked hundreds of classified government documents—an action that has been described as the largest security breach in the history of the world. Taken together, the stories related in chapters 2 through 5 provide a narrow window into the world of guerrilla government. While three of the four take place in the environmental policy arena (which is the subject of my policy expertise), similar events could take place in virtually any public organization in any country, regardless of policy area.

The first episode, concerning the "Nevada Four," surfaced as I served on a National Academy of Sciences panel concerning irrigation-induced water quality problems in the western United States. For four years we heard "gloom and doom" stories of how DOI irrigation practices were destroying the environment in nearly every regional office site in the western United States—except one in Nevada. Something just didn't ring true when the Nevada DOI employees initially testified that legislation imposed "from outside the Department" forced them to change their internal departmental policies, enabling them to implement innovations they had always dreamed of creating but could never get clearance for from their superiors. After confirming my suspicions through private conversations with one of the site's speakers, I began to investigate the real story of guerrilla government in the DOI.

The second episode, which took place in the Seattle regional office of the U.S. Environmental Protection Agency, surfaced when I was presenting my research on the DOI at the School of Public and Environmental Affairs at Indiana University, where I used to work. One of my colleagues there was a retired EPA deputy regional administrator. "Guerrilla government happens more than people will admit," he said. "Let me tell you about my own experience." His experience, and the experiences of his former colleagues at the EPA, became the core of that story.

The third episode, about off-road vehicles in the Hoosier National Forest, surfaced when I placed an ad in the national newsletter of the American Society for Public Administration's Section on Environmental and Natural Resources Administration asking for guerrilla government stories for my book. Dozens of letters poured in, with the story of Claude Ferguson and the Forest Service coming, ironically, from one of my own students who had worked for Ferguson.

It was impossible not to write about the fourth episode, the WikiLeaks scandal. When it hit the international media, I was contacted by colleagues around the world who told me that the second edition of this book would be incomplete without this case. The story related in chapter 5 is based on secondary data derived from archives, blogs, reprints of Private Manning's e-mail messages, and news accounts.

Sprinkled among the four primary case studies are interludes of vignettes or snapshots of other guerrilla government stories from outside the environmental policy arena. I offer these to provide a greater sense of the prevalence, types, and modes of guerrilla government activity happening today.

The last chapter of this book steps back from the cases and examines the phenomenon of guerrilla government and its implications. The chapter presents five harsh realities about guerrilla government and discusses ways of addressing guerrilla government, including implementing dispute system design, changing organization culture, training employees in collaborative problem solving, integrating the expressive and instrumental objectives of organizations, and training new political appointees. The chapter also presents advice gleaned from a survey of 216 organization managers and offers a vision for life "in the system" that seeks to bring government guerrillas back into the fold. Finally, a postlude asks if there are lessons to be learned from this study of guerrilla government.

NOTES

1. See Bouville 2008; Uys 2008; De Graaf 2010; Miceli, Near, Rehg, and Van Scotter 2012.

2. Aaron Wildavsky and Francis Rourke expanded the concept in the 1960s, followed by Graham Allison, Morton Halperin, and Guy Peters in the 1970s and 1980s. Hundreds of studies followed.

3. See, for example, Blau 1979; Milward 1980; West 1985, 1995; Bendor, Taylor, and Van Gaalen 1985; Gormley 1989; Cook 1996; Brehm and Gates 1997; Meier and Bohte 2006; Aberbach and Rockman 2000, 2006; Peters 2009; Howlett 2011; Howlett and Walker 2012; Witesman and Wise 2012.

4. See also Frey 1982; Near and Miceli 1986; Fitzgerald 1989; Glazer and Glazer 1989; Jos, Tompkins, and Hays 1989; Johnson and Kraft 1990; Alford, 2002, 2007; Johnson, 2003; Rothwell and Baldwin 2007; Park and Blenkinsopp 2009; Vadera, Aguilera, and Caza 2009; Vandekerckhove and Tsahuridu 2010; Kaptein 2011; and Hedin and Mansson 2012.

2

Guerrilla Government
and the Nevada Wetlands

IN THE WANING HOURS of its final session of 1990, the U.S. Congress passed the Fallon Paiute Shoshone Indian Tribes Water Rights Settlement Act. That bill, which was signed into law by President George H. W. Bush on November 16, 1990, as Public Law 101-618, represented a pathbreaking change in western irrigation policy.[1] The new law significantly addressed irrigation-induced water quality problems in several ways. First, it settled the long-debated issue of whether the U.S. Department of the Interior is permitted to buy water rights originally designated for Bureau of Reclamation irrigation projects and then use those water rights to maintain wetlands areas. The law gave the DOI this authority. Second, under the new law the secretary of the DOI was authorized to take such actions as may be necessary to prevent, correct, or mitigate adverse water quality and fish and wildlife habitat conditions attributable to agricultural drain waste originating from federal irrigation projects. Third, the law ordered the DOI to close the "TJ Drain," a major irrigation runoff pollution site in Nevada.

The bill, sponsored by Senator Harry Reid of Nevada, officially was not supported by the Department of the Interior (testimony of John Sayre, Constance Harriman, and Eddie F. Brown, assistant secretaries, DOI, February 6, 1990). The bill officially was supported, however, by a vast network made up of environmental groups, Indian tribes, chambers of commerce, hunters, trappers, and conservation groups.[2] One strand of the web that many people will never know existed was composed of career bureaucrats in the DOI and the Nevada Department of Wildlife (NDOW). These guerrillas worked behind the scenes, first to develop support for the bill before Senator Reid decided to sponsor it and later as ghostwriters of parts of the final act. At some junctures they put their jobs in jeopardy by directly disobeying their superiors and promoting policies against which their organizations argued both officially and unofficially. This is their story.

MAKING THE DESERTS BLOOM

In 1902, the United States initiated a program aimed at "making the deserts bloom." The seventeen western states were targeted for multimillion-dollar irrigation projects with the goal of bringing inexpensive water to be used for communities and for farming. Today irrigation of about fifty million acres of land consumes about 90 percent of the water in the western United States. The DOI's Bureau of Reclamation is responsible for approximately one-fourth of the nation's irrigation projects. Water quality problems associated with the DOI's irrigation projects include increased salinity, accumulation of trace elements such as selenium and boron, and accumulation of pesticides (National Research Council 1989) (see Map 2.1).

In interviews, all of the four major guerrillas in the Nevada case (hereafter referred to as the Nevada Four)[3] emphasized that they had a shared long-term goal: save the Stillwater and Carson Lake (or Lahontan Valley) wetlands from Bureau of Reclamation irrigation practices at the Nevada Newlands Project. As scientists, they had concluded that these practices had negative impacts on the environment, diverting water from the wetlands and inducing water quality problems, such as the accumulation of trace elements that can be toxic to wildlife (see Box 2.1). This goal became their number one concern, overriding other "tedious bureaucratic responsibilities" with which they felt forced to deal.[4] The goal became more important than

Map 2.1 The Lahontan Valley Wetlands

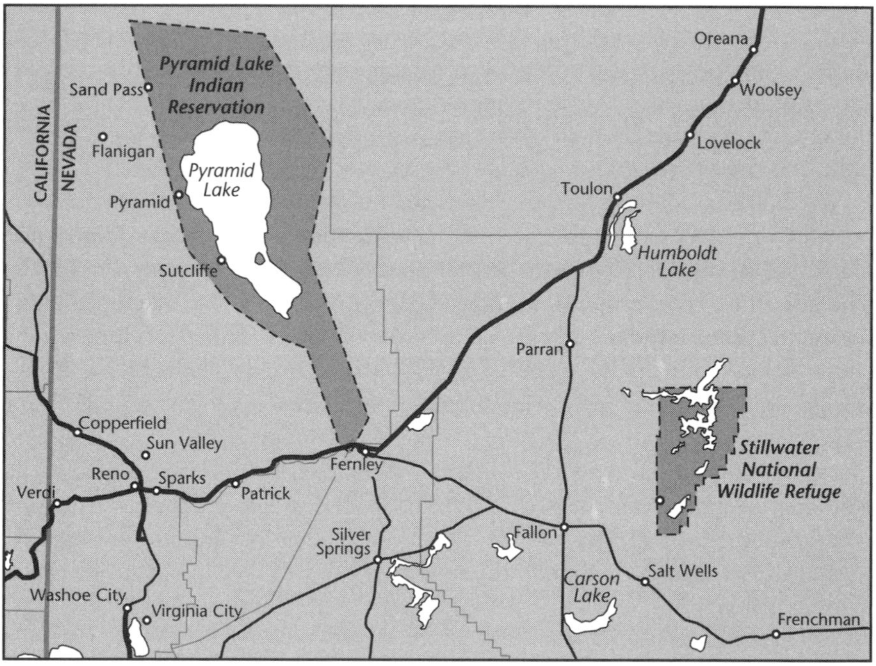

pleasing their superiors, upholding departmental policy, or appeasing potentially hostile interest groups. When asked why this goal took priority, each of the Nevada Four said, "because it was the right thing to do." Each described being driven personally, one spiritually, out of a deep concern for wildlife and a desire to "do something good for nature." Three of the four had a long-term personal connection to the area and had seen two other wildlife refuges in the area deteriorate (the Winnemucca Lake and Fallon refuges) (see Table 2.1). Others pointed out that even the U.S. Fish and Wildlife Service made things difficult by focusing primarily on endangered species at the expense of wetlands. Hence the Nevada Four's goal became that of helping the ailing wetlands by increasing the flow of water into them and cleaning up toxic sinks. If this meant changing Bureau of Reclamation policies as well as similar policies of the state of Nevada, then those changes would have to be made.

Box 2.1 The Stillwater Management Area and the U.S. Department of the Interior

The Stillwater Wildlife Management Area was established in Nevada in 1948. It comprises a waterfowl sanctuary of more than 24,000 acres. Up to 250,000 ducks, 13,000 swans, and 10,000 geese have used the area annually during wet-year spring and fall migrations. The Stillwater Wildlife Management Area and nearby Carson Lake together constitute the largest primary wetlands within the Lahontan Valley.

The U.S. Department of the Interior comprises several bureaus with conflicting missions. The Bureau of Reclamation, for example, was created in 1902 primarily to build dams, power plants, and irrigation systems. Contrasted to this is the mission of the U.S. Fish and Wildlife Service, created in part in 1871, which is "to conserve, protect, and enhance fish, wildlife, plants, and their habitats for the continuing benefit of the American people."

Sources: Anglin 1989; U.S. Fish and Wildlife Service, "Mission Statement," http://www.fws.gov/info/pocketguide/fundamentals.html.

Table 2.1 The Destruction of the Wetlands of Nevada

	Area			
	Historic Acreage	*1987 Acreage*	*Acreage Lost*	*Percent Lost*
Carson Lake	25,600	1,900–7,500	18,000	71
Stillwater	33,400	1,400–16,144	17,256	51
Fallon	26,500	0	26,500	100
Winnemucca Lake	61,515	0	61,515	100
Total	205,015	36,481	168,534	82

Source: U.S. Fish and Wildlife Service data, 1987.

At the same time, each of the Nevada Four expressed surprise at the diverse incremental steps required to reach their goal. One said that what he originally visualized as a straight line became a series of zigzags. There were many failures, benefactors who did not come through, sources of help (such as hunters and trappers) who were not initially thought to be allies, and other unanticipated sources of help and hindrance. Further, the task, in the end, proved to be more difficult and personally draining than any of them had originally anticipated. One put it this way: "If anyone told me at the beginning that this would entail over 100 interviews with reporters, over 120 newspaper articles, lobbying, report writing, forging coalitions with groups I never thought I could get along with, and four years of intense stress, I would have said, 'Forget it!'"

Right or wrong, the Nevada Four never gave up. They kept coming back despite occasional setbacks. They kept their long-range goal in mind. They had a single focus. They were going to save the Stillwater and Carson Lake wetlands.

ATTACK FROM THE OUTSIDE

The Nevada Four were convinced that attempting to change their bureaucracies from the inside would never work. The attack had to be from the outside. Their bureaucracies, they insisted, were unable to look objectively at their own problems. The most senior member of the Nevada Four talked about "banging . . . [his] head against a wall for twenty years" only to conclude that the goal of saving the wetlands would never be achieved by working within his own bureaucracy. A member of a Nevada wildlife protection group who is also a retired NDOW employee said that the Nevada Four had been "emasculated—that's the only way to put it—emasculated from speaking" internally about the wetlands. Few individuals in positions of power within the DOI and the state of Nevada, they said, considered the wetlands important.

One guerrilla stated that James Watt, former secretary of the DOI, started a trend of crippling parts of the organization by making changes that did not have to go through public review—changes that many felt violated congressional intent.[5] Therefore, forcing public review through exposure and pressure became "the only way to work." Another member of the Nevada Four put it this way, "We couldn't attack from inside the organization because we *are* the bureaucracy." Another expressed his preference for action outside the organization by saying, "In order to create the amount of change that comes from enlisting one source of support outside of the agency, we would have to enlist ten sources of support from within the agency." (It is interesting to note that, according to Vietnam War veteran and political science scholar James Pfiffner, in "normal" warfare, the U.S. armed forces strive for a ratio of three U.S. soldiers to every one enemy soldier. In guerrilla warfare, however, the ratio is ten to one—the ratio the Nevada Four felt they needed to change policies from within their own bureaucracy.)[6] Another of the Nevada Four stated: "If you don't work outside the bureaucratic box, either you're going to be unhappy or you're stupid. When your boss ties your hands and you can't get permission to do the right thing, the only other option is mutiny."

When attacking the bureaucracy from the outside, however, one must understand one's adversary, three of the Nevada Four emphasized. Know the enemy. One put it this way, "Know who is playing the game and their source of power. Otherwise you'll get stabbed in the back."

MARKETING THEIR CAUSE

The Nevada Four were successful in developing grassroots support for saving the wetlands partially because they deliberately developed that support. Put another way, they aggressively marketed their issue. They initiated Saturday-morning "doughnut tours" of the wetlands to educate citizens. They put together a slide show and arranged for an elected official to sponsor the presentation at the local Rotary Club, briefing him the hour before with "smart questions" he could ask and insightful points he could make. They drafted press releases that ended up on the UPI wire service. More than 120 articles about the wetlands were published in newspapers, including *USA Today* and the *New York Times*. One author described the media reaction this way: "The media response to efforts to publicize the plight of Stillwater was immediate and prolonged. Articles in major national newspapers and magazines and programs on national, regional, and local television programs made Stillwater a *cause celebre*" (Strickland 1992). Reporters were invited to tour the wildlife refuge and often gave the staff there tips about how to get the maximum amount of press coverage. The Nevada Four granted all requests for media interviews and handed out to interviewers summaries of the most salient points about the wetlands to help promote accurate reporting. At times they told reporters, "Here's the story, but don't quote me." These confidences were always kept. The public servants also learned to answer the questions of reporters who didn't quite understand what the Nevada Four wanted them to know by gently pulling them verbally in a specific direction.

The Nevada Four distributed gruesome photographs of fish kills and deformed birds. They targeted aggressive young reporters "on the way up—rising stars" and fed them information. More than one of the Nevada Four described the process as "manipulating the press." Local television stations in Reno and San Francisco sponsored a series of multinight news specials titled "Death in the Refuge" and "Wildlife Disaster." This television coverage was picked up by CBS, ABC, and CNN. Pieces of the television specials were consolidated into a video, two hundred copies of which were distributed. More than thirty radio programs devoted time to discussion of the wetlands. Briefing books with simple one-line explanations of key points were assembled for legislators. Guided airboat and airplane rides were arranged. These public employees, trained as natural scientists, became experts in public relations.

"If you don't contact the media," one member of the Nevada Four explained, "nothing will happen." He then offered advice for all concerned public managers: "Get to know reporters. Establish personal contact with them. Get them to trust you and vice versa. Send them blind carbon copies of everything you do."

"It got to the point where I concluded that being right was not enough," another of the Nevada Four said. "We had to convince others that we were right." When later asked if they had seized a "window of opportunity," one responded, "Window? Hell no, we built the house. We started with the foundation, then built the structure, then the walls, the windows and the roof. Each press release, each contact with an interest group, each discussion with an elected official was a brick in the house." Another emphasized the importance of developing support from the bottom. Only with this support could they gain enough power to overrule the policies of what he called "Mr. Big," the government.

NATIONAL WETLANDS POLICY

The Nevada Four's window of opportunity was a growing national interest in wetlands. During the 1988 presidential election campaign, candidate George H. W. Bush called for "no net loss of wetlands" (BNA *Environment Reporter,* September 16, 1988). One month later, a national wetlands policy forum convened by the Conservation Foundation released more than one hundred recommendations for protecting wetlands (BNA *Environment Reporter,* November 18, 1988). Many of those recommendations became legislation that was hotly debated in Congress. In January 1989, the DOI published a document that detailed the destruction of wetlands by federal programs.

At the same time, Bureau of Reclamation projects continued to destroy thousands of acres of wetlands (National Research Council 1989). The Nevada Four pointed out these inconsistencies at every opportunity. The contrast was enough to gain widespread attention for the plight of the wetlands.

A CRISIS EMERGES

In the spring of 1987, a crisis hit the Stillwater Wildlife Refuge: an estimated 7.5 million tui chub fish were found dead. At first no one was certain what had caused the deaths, but one of the Nevada Four, seeing an opportunity for national attention, pounced and, in the words of one of his colleagues, "played it to the hilt." Pictures of the fish kill were distributed, and reporters across the nation were called and invited to the refuge to see the problem.

In the subsequent interviews, the Nevada Four emphasized that the cause of the deaths was unknown, but one possibility was selenium toxicosis associated with the drainage of some Bureau of Reclamation irrigation projects. Selenium toxicosis had been the diagnosis at the Kesterson Wildlife Refuge in California, where thousands of birds and other wildlife had died from such poisoning in the early 1980s (Harris 1991). One San Francisco television reporter said during an evening newscast that the Stillwater situation could be "twenty times worse than Kesterson" if not treated (Davis 1987a). The Kesterson nightmare was a national controversy that the DOI and the NDOW did not want repeated in Nevada.

It was later discovered that the fish kill was not caused by selenium toxicosis. Ironically, it was caused at least in part by a previous high-water year at the refuge. Carson sink had become naturally high, causing an explosive increase in the number of fish. When the water receded, the fish died from low-dissolved oxygen in the water as well as from stress caused by a tough winter. By the time the reasons for the fish kill were determined, however, the Stillwater Wildlife Refuge had received coverage on the front pages of many U.S. newspapers, in a German newspaper, and on the evening news broadcasts of several major television networks.

The Nevada Four used this crisis—as well as other crises, such as one that occurred when hundreds of birds, including two bald eagles, died prematurely—as an opportunity to get their agenda on the table of policy makers and as a "decisive trigger." (The concept of a decisive trigger, which comes from social learning theory [Bandura 1978], holds that individuals usually must be able to perceive a problem vividly before they will address it.) "Things had to get bad before anyone would do anything," a member of an environmental group explained. The fish kill, then, became more a symbol of a threat than an actual threat.

LOBBYING STRATEGY

The Nevada Four lobbied on behalf of their own programs. This lobbying took several forms, including state, national, government, and public interest group contacts. They utilized all their local contacts: friends, relatives, anyone who had a connection with state legislators. One of the four had a family friend who was a state legislator as well as an uncle whose cousin was in the state legislature, for example. These people were helpful in spearheading support for a wildlife initiative that was passed by Nevada voters by a margin of two to one on November 6, 1990, making $5 million to $9 million available for the acquisition of water rights for Stillwater and other Nevada wetlands (Strickland 1992).

When a U.S. senator was heard on the radio proposing that $1.2 million be earmarked for dikes for the refuge that, in the opinion of the Nevada Four, were not needed, the guerrillas telephoned the senator and invited him to tour the refuge. Telling their superiors in Washington that the senator had requested the tour, the guerrillas took him out in an airboat and convinced him that the money he had proposed for dikes could be better used to buy water rights for the refuge. The senator was successful in redirecting the funds to the purchase of water rights. This was the first time Congress had appropriated funds from a federal irrigation project for the acquisition of water to be used for wetlands (Strickland 1992).

Some of the Nevada Four flew to Washington and met with congressional aides. "You'd be surprised how much access the average citizen has in Washington," exclaimed one of the Nevada Four. Another emphasized that he worked only with staff, not the elected officials themselves, because of his fear that his actions might come to the attention of his DOI superiors.

Staff from some congressional offices flew to Nevada to meet with members of the Nevada Four. Several people recall fondly a night at a Basque restaurant in Reno, where the wetlands sections of the final Senate bill were sketched out on napkins. A map of the affected wetlands, for the bill, also was drawn up that night. The same persons involved in that meeting cooperated to write a section of the bill that mandated the closure of the TJ Drain, a toxic runoff site on Indian land. Some of the Nevada Four had tried to shut down the site previously but had been unable to obtain permission from their superiors to do so.

Other meetings involving congressional staff and members of the Nevada Four are documented in the minutes of the Lahontan Valley Wetlands Coalition (LVWC). The August 1988 minutes, for example, mention such a meeting that also included members of the media. The following issues were discussed:

- How could one force the Bureau of Reclamation to implement the Fish and Wildlife Coordination Act?
- Was it possible to obtain more funds for Stillwater?
- Could funds be obtained from the Bureau of Reclamation?

At one point Senator Reid himself was given a tour of the wildlife refuge.

The Nevada Four also lobbied members of environmental groups such as the Environmental Defense Fund (EDF) and the Sierra Club. These lobbying activities took two forms. The first primarily involved members of the Nevada Four meeting with representatives of these groups in Washington, D.C. The guerrillas arrived armed with a video of soaring white pelicans at Pyramid Lake, Nevada, with New Age music playing in the background, to give the environmentalists what one of the four called "warm fuzzies." Because of the great personal expense of such trips, however, the Nevada Four also pursued a second avenue. In one instance, when they were in San Francisco on an official government business trip, they arranged to participate in a wine and cheese reception at the EDF office. During the reception, they discussed saving the wetlands. Several EDF staff members expressed an interest in helping, and new partnerships were forged.

FUND-RAISING

At the Nevada Newlands irrigation site, neither the DOI nor the NDOW owned water rights, in contrast to some other DOI irrigation projects. This yielded a situation in which, as one of the Nevada Four put it, "the Indians had water rights, the farmers had water rights, the city of Reno had water rights, the developers had water rights. Everyone and everything seemed to have water rights except the wetlands." Outraged by an attorney's statement that the wetlands were a "bunch of parasites" because the only water they received was runoff from irrigation, and concerned with the lack of water reaching the wetlands because of a drought that began in 1987 (plus measures to conserve water used in farming), one of the Nevada Four took action. He checked the files of the Truckee-Carson Irrigation District and developed a list of more than 1,200 holders of water rights who were not using those rights. He then contacted a certified public accountant and obtained a statement that the donation of water rights is tax deductible. The owners of the inactive water rights then were contacted and asked to donate their water rights to the wetlands. Forty people initially donated nearly 130 acre-feet of water. "This blew everything out of the water," exclaimed the public employee who initiated this action. "The rules of the game had changed. The old ways of operating no longer applied. We had shown that it was now possible to dedicate water rights solely to the wetlands." This sort of "thinking outside the box," they felt, would never be allowed within the DOI.

Since that time, the Nevada Waterfowl Association has held dances and other fund-raising events; one of the association's founding fathers is a member of the Nevada Four. A newsletter published by the LVWC reported on the success of the first fund-raiser:

> The wetlands barbecue on August 21 at the Elks Club was a resounding success. The final accounting is not complete but Nevada Waterfowl Association estimates that approximately $22,000 may have been netted. As a first event for a new organization, in fact two new organizations, the Nevada Waterfowl Association was founded a year ago; the Lahontan Valley Wetlands Coalition in March, this is phenomenal. Almost 400 tickets were sold in a little under four weeks. The smooth functioning of the raffle, the auction, ticket sales, and the excellent barbecue, is a tribute to . . . members who volunteered their time and expertise to the event. (September 1990)

The Sierra Club made an initial donation of $2,000 (Strickland 1992). More than $100,000 was raised in this fashion and used to purchase water rights for the wetlands. One of the Nevada Four later obtained a donation from the Nevada Mining Association to be used for this purpose.

Droughts and protracted legal fights over water had discouraged some farmers in Nevada. Aware that many wanted to leave farming, the Nevada Waterfowl Association was happy to help them out: the association purchased unproductive farms solely to gain their water rights. (One news announcer analogized this action to buying a bar to obtain the liquor [Davis 1987b].) The land was then sold to city dwellers who want weekend retreats and to local residents who are able to tap into underground wells to meet their basic water consumption needs. The

Conservation Foundation and the Environmental Defense Fund helped with the legal work associated with the purchase of the water rights. By spring 1993, approximately 50 percent of the water rights for land irrigated by the Newlands Project in Nevada had been purchased under this program.[7]

EMBARRASSING THE GOVERNMENT

Despite the impressive amounts of money raised privately for the wetlands, one of the Nevada Four insisted that the real value of such action was in "embarrassing the government," particularly the DOI. He put it this way:

> For years they told us the wetlands had no rights. For years they told us that nothing could be done to protect them. For years they refused to give us the money we needed to do our job right. For years we were told that there was not enough support to request funds to save the wetlands. We showed them. We showed them that there *is* support out there among the average Joe Citizen.

Embarrassing the government—both the bureaucracy that the Nevada Four had been fighting for years and the politicians—brought a sense of vindication. Outside sources not only agreed with the public servants but also were willing to put money behind them. The fact that many of the outside forces were associated with conservation groups was also an important message to send "Mr. Big," the Nevada Four said. Further, the Nevada Four had sent a message to their own bureaucracies that they were a force to be reckoned with and could no longer be ignored.

NETWORK MANAGEMENT

The list of groups with which the Nevada Four linked up (sometimes formally, but usually informally) to form alliances is a long one. It includes the Reno Chamber of Commerce, the Pyramid Lake Paiute Indian Tribe, the Fallon Paiute-Shoshone Indian Tribe, the Truckee-Carson Irrigation District, the Nevada Waterfowl Association, Ducks Unlimited, the Nevada Organization for Wildlife, the Canvasback Club, the Greenhead Hunting Club, the Ormsby Sportsmen Association, Defenders of Wildlife, the Nevada Trappers Association, Friends of Pyramid Lake, the Environmental Defense Fund, the Sierra Club, the Conservation Foundation, the Audubon Society, the Humane Society, and the Nevada Wildlife Federation. In some instances these groups, such as those that made up the Lahontan Valley Wetlands Coalition, were begun by others who turned to the Nevada Four for help in understanding the science behind the problem. While the two founders of the LVWC gained national prominence by winning the prestigious Chevron Conservation Award (Tina Nappe) and a Sierra Club Award (Rose Strickland) for their work on the Nevada wetlands, the minutes of the twice-a-month meetings of the LVWC show that the Nevada Four provided crucial scientific information in support of the coalition's efforts.

The minutes of the November 29, 1988, meeting of the LVWC, for example, show that eight DOI employees gave presentations concerning the possibility of purchasing water rights for the wetlands, while the minutes of the November 10, 1988, meeting document collaboration of the Nevada Four with members of the Nature Conservancy. Minutes of the January 12, 1989, meeting document the coauthorship by one of the Nevada Four of the LVWC's testimony for a legislative meeting with a member of the Sierra Club. The minutes of a June 1990 meeting of the LVWC thank two of the Nevada Four for their help. The minutes describe one as "a 22 year employee of the Nevada Department of Wildlife whose knowledge of and concern for both the wetlands and the residents of Fallon [Nevada] have made him a key player in wetlands preservation." "Both employees," the minutes continue, "have volunteered many hours to meet with interested groups and provide technical information needed to make informed decisions." Both were honored "for outstanding service to wetlands" at a June 1990 dinner sponsored by the LVWC. At an Audubon Society conference, a member of the LVWC referred to the Nevada Four as "the greatest repository of knowledge" for the environmental group (Nappe 1989).

One member of the Sierra Club, calling the Nevada Four "unsung heroes," said that they gave the LVWC data before the data had been published by the DOI. She continued:

> Ironically, those data landed on the front page of *USA Today*. . . . We couldn't have done it without them. . . . They performed the highest form of service to their country [by helping us]. . . . At the same time, they were just as desperate as we were. They were not solving their problems alone. We helped each other out.

The desperation of the Nevada Four that drove them to forge coalitions with interest groups outside their organizations also was mentioned in a paper presented at an Audubon Society conference; the author described the government workers as in "high distress but limited as to how their anguish could be funneled" (Nappe 1989). An article by one of the LVWC's founders heralded the efforts of the Nevada Four:

> Hunters and conservationists alike were impressed by the dedication and personal commitment of agency wildlife biologists who not only provided critical technical information but volunteered countless hours in fundraising and other organizational needs of the Coalition. (Strickland 1992)

As mentioned previously, one member of the Nevada Four was also a founding member of another group that assisted in building support for the wetlands. That group, the Nevada Waterfowl Association, was composed primarily of hunters who saw the demise of the wetlands as the demise of their hunting grounds. While the group officially was headed by a local dentist, the Nevada Four member served as ghostwriter, composing letters to politicians, Nevada officials, and DOI officials that the dentist would then sign. Another member of the association had a friend who worked in the White House and who proved to be a valuable ally.

Each group with which the Nevada Four worked was an important strand in the spiderweb—or network—underlying the Reid bill. Each provided different sources of credibility and support. Often, however, no progress was made until the members of the Nevada Four had met three or four times with individual groups. One of the four described this process as "uncomfortable":

> It's uncomfortable to seek out people who are not just like you. It's uncomfortable to expose yourself in public. It's uncomfortable to reach out to your enemies and then sit there and have them scream at you for three hours. But after all the screaming, those who stick around are there to help. And to those who leave you can always say, "You were invited and you didn't give us any ideas."

Once they had established a positive relationship with a group, the Nevada Four sent the group's members copies of key biological assessments documenting the degradation of the wetlands. When asked why these linkages were so successful, one put it this way:

> I would always try to establish a common ground with people to let them know "we're just like you." Find out what they like to do. Invite them to tour the refuge, or go fishing, or go golfing. Anything to get over the feeling that "you are my enemy." I cannot emphasize enough how important it was to find common interests, establish *personal* contacts with individuals.

It also was important to let those individuals know that their expertise was respected, one said.

Personal relationships were important in other ways as well. One contact at the U.S. Environmental Protection Agency was developed when an EPA employee came to the refuge to bird-watch. Another contact at the Council on Environmental Quality developed similarly. These personal contacts often paid off in terms of information tips. At one juncture, for example, a farmer whose support had been cultivated but who had decided not to sign up officially as an ally called one of the Nevada Four to warn him that he was about to "get the shaft" from a DOI manager. The tip was fed to environmental interest groups, such as the LVWC, which then successfully attacked the DOI hierarchy and protected the lower-level DOI employee.

One common theme in many of the guidelines discussed above is the building of partnerships with nongovernment people and associations. For example, the Nevada Four asked the Environmental Defense Fund and the Nature Conservancy for assistance. The strategy articulated by one of the Nevada Four included looking for "young and aggressive upstarts" in these organizations who were either "on their way up" or trying to find ways to "make a name" for themselves. By selling the importance of the issue to these handpicked dynamos, the Nevada Four developed powerful allies. As mentioned previously, public-private partnerships provided the initial catalyst for the idea that water rights could be purchased for the wetlands.

Tied in with this, the Nevada Four had no time for intergovernmental turf fights for several reasons. First, since they hoped to hide most of their actions from those at higher levels in their hierarchies, they could not afford to take credit for successes. None of the four was interested in becoming a sacrificial lamb. In fact, one stressed the importance of giving others outside the government credit for any success. Second, they were dedicated to a goal, not to personal aggrandizement. Protection of the wetlands came first. As one put it: "We could either spit in the wind or cooperate with each other. We did not have the luxury of *not* agreeing—or not working together. The protection of resources was the point, not power." Third, they were located in a rural area where people knew their neighbors. They were friends. Their children went to school together. Personal connections helped keep turf fights from developing.

Finally, this intergovernmental cooperation paid off financially. As noted above, money for the wetlands was obtained not only from the federal government and private individuals but also from the Nevada legislature.

RISK TAKING

At times, members of the Nevada Four put their jobs on the line. One recalled an incident when two of them had been asked by a superior to change a scientific report that concluded that Bureau of Reclamation practices would result in an annual average loss of about 15,000 acres of wetlands. He expressed his inner turmoil:

> I never thought it would be that difficult [to say no]. I sat there and thought about the $400 I had in my savings account in the bank, about how I was going to support my children. . . . As a family we were really stretched out [financially]. . . . It was a lot harder than I ever thought it would be to go that final step. I was real scared. In the end, however, I figured if you give in, they've got you.

He decided to tell his superior that he would reconsider his data, and then he came back with a stronger report concluding that the proposed Bureau of Reclamation practices would result in a loss of "roughly 17,000–18,000 acres of wetlands." He gave the report to a friend at the EPA, who forwarded it to the EPA regional director, who in turn contacted the DOI to express his dismay.

At other times subtler threats were made by superiors who discovered the Nevada Four's guerrilla activities. For example, DOI employees were asked if they liked Puerto Rican rum, a not-so-veiled threat to have them sent to the DOI wildlife refuges in Puerto Rico, which were considered the worst assignments in the department. On other wildlife refuges, three employees were moved to less appealing assignments because of their opposition to official DOI policies (Harris 1991). These actions were talked about a lot, with the implied threat being "Clean up your act or this could be you." "It was very intimidating," one of the Nevada Four admitted. "The government punishes risk takers."

"Your whole life can't be centered around a paycheck," explained another of the Nevada Four. "Money isn't the point. You have to follow higher values and be willing to take risks for those values."

SCIENTIFIC KNOWLEDGE

The Nevada Four's strong suit was their scientific knowledge. Each was trained as a biologist. Each emphasized that at every juncture they had to be certain about the biological facts in order to maintain professional credibility. While they were willing to think politically and use related crises to their advantage, they maintained that they would point out the *possible* source of the problem only if all facts were not known. It was their allegiance to science that they perceived to carry them through the most difficult challenges. Factual information, they all agreed, was the key to their success. Despite the irony of the false selenium toxicosis scare, one had this advice for other career public workers: "People who want to do what we do have to be sure they're right. Don't get on thin ice. If you're wrong about your facts, you're dead."

DOWNSIDE

One might get the impression that the Nevada Four were oblivious to the negative views of many within their organization. Nothing could be further from the truth. Trained as biologists, they were often ostracized for going against the scientific or political conclusions of their peers, for not following standard operating procedures, or for violating the norms of the Department of the Interior. Some colleagues refused to speak with them, apparently afraid they would be deemed guilty by association. One said he felt as if he had come down with "an instant case of leprosy." When the Nevada Four attended meetings with groups that they had formerly thought of as "the enemy," some other government workers called the four "traitors."

Other colleagues were helpful, but only in after-hours phone calls at home or unsigned notes sent in envelopes with no return addresses. While some superiors supported the Nevada Four behind the scenes, this support was rarely made public. One of the four described being yelled at in a meeting, only to have his boss pull him aside later, wink, and say, "Keep going." Another had what he called "close to a nervous breakdown" in the middle of the battle; he became completely paralyzed, his body "just shut down for three months." All described loss of time with their families and enormous stress. One of the Nevada Four described his loneliness in this way:

> It's as if there's this Mr. Big out there telling you not to do the right thing. There is an immense amount of career pressure. Don't go against Mr. Big or you will pay. We went against Mr. Big, and although we beat those bastards, we paid a heavy price.

EPILOGUE

Twenty-three years after the passage of Public Law 101-618, close to 30,000 acre-feet of water rights have been purchased in fifty transactions. Partners include the Nature Conservancy, the state of Nevada, the U.S. Fish and Wildlife Service, and the Nevada Waterfowl Association. Total realization of the dream to save the wetlands has been delayed by prolonged drought and the arrival of a new manager of the Stillwater National Wildlife Area who disagreed with the guerrilla government actions of the Nevada Four.

NOTES

1. The law also settled one hundred years of litigation over water rights in Nevada and California. For a summary of those portions of the law, see Rusco 1992.

2. Other scholars have referred to similar "webs" as issue networks (Heclo 1978), policy networks (Rhodes and Marsh 1992), regulatory communities (Meidinger, personal communication, 1992), and "spiderwebs" (O'Leary 1994).

3. It should be noted that there were additional bureaucratic players behind the scenes who worked on the Reid bill. The minutes of the meetings of the Lahontan Valley Wetlands Coalition, for example, document the participation of twelve additional DOI staff and five additional NDOW employees.

4. All quotes from those involved in this case are from 1991 interviews unless otherwise noted.

5. These actions by Watt were confirmed in accounts published in the environmental press (BNA *Environment Reporter,* May 13, 1983, 55; BNA *Environment Reporter,* June 22, 1984, 298; BNA *Environment Reporter,* October 12, 1984, 956).

6. Comments of Pfiffner at the National Conference of the American Political Science Association, fall 1992.

7. This purchase of water rights only from willing sellers, as mandated by the Reid bill, has yielded the negative consequence of a checkerboard pattern of farms that are irrigated and farms that are not. Some fear that this will eventually yield a situation where water will have to travel long distances only to serve one or two farms, with water being wasted and possibly polluted as it flows through unlined canals.

First Interlude:
More Stories of Guerrilla
Government

I SENT AN E-MAIL MESSAGE to former graduate students who now work in government, asking if they had any guerrilla government stories to share. Here are some of the best responses.

GUERRILLA GOVERNMENT
IN THE MEDICAL FIELD

I was the administrative director of the department of surgery in a large medical school. My boss was chair of the department. It was a huge department comprising several divisions (e.g., plastic surgery, neurosurgery), several hospitals, residency programs, and more. There was a lot of vying for power. It was very hierarchical and sexist. It was an organizational culture that subverted the truth.

My boss hired a new chair of one of the divisions, "Dr. Wood." After several years of doing surgery at the medical center, several doctors noticed that the mentally handicapped patients upon whom Dr. Wood operated were dying in his operating rooms at an alarming rate.

Two doctors went to the chair of the department and revealed their concerns. The chair said that their claims were ridiculous and that he would have no part of their discussions. His view was "I'm the chair . . . don't you dare question me!!" He wasn't looking for the truth; he was looking for blind obedience. Also, because he was supposed to be godlike, in hindsight I can see that he felt he couldn't admit that he made a huge mistake by hiring Dr. Wood, even though patients were not being cared for appropriately. This triggered a lot of hurt, angst, and dissention.

About this time I invited the two concerned doctors and their wives to my home for dinner. By the end of the evening, the conversation turned to their suspicions about Dr. Wood. One of the doctors revealed that he knew Dr. Wood in the army and that he thought he was a very sick human being. All of us thought that Dr. Wood was strange from the beginning. My gut told me that there was something seriously wrong here.

That night we agreed that I would help by going into the records room to obtain the records of Dr. Wood's patients. We felt we had to work clandestinely because the chair had said no to cooperating with the surgeons who were worried about patient care. We thought that there was no other channel or avenue to pursue. We suspected that the records, when looked at as a whole, would indicate how he treated the patients and who died. Our plan was to put together a chain of evidence to prove a pattern of malpractice.

This was seriously difficult. It took about a year, but we had appropriate documents in the end. Eventually Dr. Wood was fired. He was sent to rehab and ordered to operate only when someone else was with him. We never heard of him again.

Today this probably wouldn't happen with outcomes measures, oversight, and with doctors working more in teams. Today we also have conferences where they beat on the residents to try to avoid situations like this. If we had an anonymous hotline, the capacity to send anonymous e-mail messages, a sympathetic dean we could go to, or an oversight committee to talk with, then we wouldn't have had to do this clandestinely. One person does not have that much power today.

I know I did the right thing. I worshipped my boss, but it wasn't even difficult to do this behind his back. We were talking about patients' lives. And I trusted the two younger surgeons who had confided in me. This was an enormous issue for me. I was at the highest grade at the university under assistant professors and I easily could have lost my job. But if I had it to do it over again the truth is I would have done it earlier, more openly, and more of it if needed.

PREVENTING GUERRILLA GOVERNMENT IN A NATIONAL HEALTH INSURANCE ORGANIZATION

I am a senior vice president for a national health insurance organization. One of the major concerns of management in our organization is that there must exist adequate channels for employee dissent, comments, and concerns so they don't feel they need to act clandestinely as "guerrillas." We have built a very costly infrastructure in an attempt to provide avenues for employees to voice their viewpoints and to bring to light any wrongdoing. Our belief is that a concerned or disgruntled employee should first talk with their immediate supervisor. If that doesn't work, we have numerous alternative options, including an anonymous hotline, anonymous e-mails, and other avenues to provide anonymous tips. I have a database full of examples; here are two stories from that database.

In one case, a female employee continually saw a manager viewing pornography on his computer at work. She went to her supervisor three times to report what she saw. Her superior's response was "This is what guys do." After being rebuffed by her superior, the female employee called our hotline. We didn't waste any time. We went in at night to look at his hard drive and disks. As it turns out, there were twenty-three disks full of porn on his desk. The porn guy was terminated and the superior who ignored the female employee also was terminated.

In a second case, a senior-level person who was of great value to the company wanted to resolve her husband's insurance claim. But there was no authorization in his file. She bullied a subordinate customer service representative, trying to convince her to give her authorization, but the subordinate refused. The senior-level person then had someone call the customer service line for her, requesting authorization. The employee on the phone asked for the birth date, which is a fraud prevention question. The person who called in could not answer the question. Amazingly, out of a possible 600 customer service phone reps, this was the same person the senior-level manager had tried to bully before. The customer service rep turned in the senior-level manager through one of our regular channels to report fraud or abuse. By the way, this case made its way all the way up to the CEO. The CEO came to me and pushed and prodded me, wanting me to back down since the senior-level person was highly valued in the company. I did not back down. The senior-level manager was fired.

Guerrilla activity typically happens when there is a lack of trust, fear of retaliation, and when employees are rebuffed by superiors. They push back.

Our dissent channels are very costly. They are frills that no one wants, so people try to cut them from the budget. But they are so important. Things can easily go amok, so you really need to manage dissent. With the private sector doing so much of the public work through contracting out these days, without adequate safeguards we will have really serious problems.

GUERRILLA GOVERNMENT IN RADAR SUPPORT

I am a field support team leader with a large federal agency and a member of the leadership development group. In the late 1980s my agency started implementing a high-tech radar network for weather (e.g., tornados, hurricanes, tsunamis) that encompassed 158 radar systems at 300 sites. Our 7,500 clients included organizations and people around the world, with our largest clients being the National Weather Service, the Federal Aviation Administration, and the Department of Defense. As part of this network, we staffed a help desk twenty-four hours a day, seven days a week in case any of the radar systems experienced trouble. This was needed given the fact that our different clients were in different time zones.

Once the radar network was complete in the 1990s, for organizational survival purposes, some managers within the organizations thought the funds previously allocated for radar should be transferred to other new projects. Therefore, I was ordered to "down-staff" the help desk; it no longer would be staffed 24/7. Instead, at times (e.g., 2:00 A.M. in the United States), if someone called in from the other side of the world they would have to wait either until the staff came on board in the morning or until a staff member could be roused out of bed.

This change in policy concerned me for three reasons. First, no impact analysis was done. Second, our clients were not asked for input. Third, there was no plan to tell our clients of this change—they would just discover it for themselves if they called in for assistance at the "wrong" time. I was told to "just do it and see if anyone yells."

I tried to present the problems of down-staffing to management but I was routinely ignored. My view was, and still is, that since I am closer to the customer than management, I could see the negative impact this would have on our clients. Management was out of touch with the customer and could not see the negative impact on our clients. I am closer to where "the agency meets the road," but there was no way to communicate upward to decision makers. I felt that this could be a potentially life-or-death situation. I felt desperate and struggled with what was the right thing to do.

Therefore, I had a robot send out e-mail messages to all 7,500 customers saying, "Effective _____ [date] there will be no support from _____ [time] to _____ [time]." While management was angry, this was nothing compared to the powerful outcry from our clients! Eventually upper-level management reversed the decision. The customers were pleased and the greater good was served.

I am dedicated to what we do here. Sending the e-mails didn't help me, but it was the right thing to do. While I was cut out of the management loop and my career was sidetracked, I have no regrets. I took a pretty big hit for doing it, but if I had to, I'd do it all over again.

This could have been prevented if management had more of a frontline perspective. Management needs to raise their head up from what they are doing on a day-to-day basis and listen to the staff who are serving the clients. Much could be learned from examining how private-sector leaders serve their global clients. I am dedicated to promoting excellence in supporting our customers.

GUERRILLA GOVERNMENT IN REGULATION PROMULGATION

When I left my JD/MPA program I had an idealistic approach to government and a sense of what should happen. I've learned that things in the real world of government are not like that.

I work for a large federal regulatory agency. I was one of seven attorneys working on the promulgation of a new regulation that would have a substantial economic impact on the entities we regulate. This regulation would set operating standards for those we regulate. That regulation had to be beyond reproach.

Knowing that I was trained in cost-benefit analysis, management asked me to analyze the impact of the rules on the regulated entities. My agency has an Office of Economic Analysis, but they weren't asked for their input.

Management asked staff for recommendations concerning whether the entities we regulate should be contacted and given an opportunity for input before the regulation was written. My recommendation was yes. I wanted to contact those affected by this new regulation in order to obtain their view of the perceived costs and to better understand how their organizations run. This was important to the development of a balanced and fair regulation.

My boss, a lawyer with no training in economics, made the decision *not* to contact these groups. He didn't want the regulated entities to know what was coming. He also didn't want on the record the regulated entities' "inflated estimates" of how much it would cost them to comply with the new regulation. Management did not want to inflame or incite folks. Basically there were a lot of political fears. Ironically, the head of our organization had already announced that the reg was coming in a speech he made at a national conference, but that didn't matter to my boss.

To me, this was a big mistake. You can't get to the heart of a problem if you don't understand the problem. You can't understand the problem unless you have the best available data. I wanted to do the most professional job possible. My thinking was that I could do a better job with better information.

Despite my superior's orders, I called or e-mailed each of the regulated entities asking for information. "I am currently working on a cost-benefit analysis of this proposed regulation," I said. "Please provide any information that would be helpful to us." I received helpful information from them, and, thankfully, no one in my group found out what I did.

What should my boss have done? Don't ask for your attorneys' advice and then disregard it. Follow staff's recommendations. More importantly, use your own Office of Economic Analysis. Obtain the input of those most affected by the regulations.

If I could do it over again, I would voice my concern to my boss's superior, the head of our department. But I didn't feel I could do that at the time because I was a probationary employee for one year and I could be fired at will.

3

Guerrilla Government
in the EPA's Seattle
Regional Office

WHEN RONALD REAGAN was elected president of the United States in 1980 he sought to make dramatic changes in the federal government. Lash, Gillman, and Sheridan (1984) sum up Reagan's mission and purpose as follows:

> He believed simply that government should spend less, do less, and interfere less with private enterprise. For 25 years since he began to make his living and his reputation as a conservative lecturer, Ronald Reagan had spent his time among those who argued there was too much government. He believed government was in the hands of people who "think control is better than freedom." He believed the bureaucrats had shackled American industry through regulation. "There are," Reagan said, "tens of thousands of . . . regulations I'd like to see eliminated." (xi–xii)

Lash et al. further note, "In his inaugural address Reagan said 'Government is not the solution to our problem; government is the problem'" (13).

Reagan appointed Anne Gorsuch administrator of the U.S. Environmental Protection Agency. In her testimony before the Senate Committee on Environment and Public Works during her confirmation hearing, Gorsuch stated: "The President is committed to regulatory reform and . . . I share [that] commitment. . . . There is no greater opportunity to effectuate that goal than the one ahead at EPA" (U.S. Senate, 96th Cong., 2d Sess., 1980). Reagan and Gorsuch implemented that quest by handpicking regional administrators for the EPA who had beliefs that matched theirs. One of these was Gorsuch's good friend John Spencer. His appointment and the later appointment of Robie Russell serve as examples of both the subtle and sophisticated power of guerrilla government and some conditions under which guerrilla government might emerge.

JOHN SPENCER AND
THE REIGN OF TERROR, 1981–1983

On August 3, 1981, John R. Spencer became the administrator of the EPA's Seattle regional office, which oversees Region 10, encompassing Alaska, Idaho, Oregon, and Washington State. Prior to his EPA appointment Spencer worked as the executive manager of municipal utilities in Anchorage, Alaska. He also was a former city attorney as well as a former vice president of RCA Alaska Communications, Inc. Upon his appointment, he assured the public that he would foster a "pragmatic response" to pollution problems and called for an end to "regulation for regulation's sake" (UPI, April 2, 1983). To top EPA career public servants in Region 10 he announced that his approach would be "management by stark terror."[1]

Spencer's tenure as EPA Region 10 administrator will long be remembered for several of the actions he took. First, he announced plans to buy, with taxpayers' money, an official membership for the EPA in the Chamber of Commerce (UPI, November 6, 1981), an organization active in lobbying before both the EPA and state environmental agencies (Clines and Weinraub 1981). He was repeatedly told by career staff in the Region 10 Management Division that this expenditure was not allowable under federal guidelines, but he continued to pursue the matter. Only after U.S. Representative Toby Moffett (D-Connecticut) blasted the move as raising "serious conflict-of-interest questions affecting the entire agency's decision-making processes" and environmentalists objected that the EPA was "paying to get in bed with big business" (UPI, November 12, 1981) did Spencer drop the idea.

According to career public servants in the Region 10 office at the time, Spencer also allegedly took some trips at public expense that were not clearly related to government activities. It appeared that Spencer made some of these trips to conclude personal business from his previous job in Alaska. He also asked for a personal driver to be assigned to him on a full-time basis and sought modifications to the EPA office building without first getting the approval of the General Services Administration as mandated by federal law. A staff member filed an anonymous complaint with the EPA Inspector General's Office concerning these alleged improprieties. (The Office of the Inspector General conducts audits, investigations, and evaluations of agency activities in an effort to improve agency performance and prevent fraud and abuse.)

When the director of the Management Division (see Box 3.1 for his résumé) heard about the complaint to the Inspector General's Office, he did nothing, contrary to Spencer's wishes. As the director told me:

> He [Spencer] held me responsible for . . . [the complaint to the inspector general]. I didn't know who did it and I didn't want to know who did it. I viewed that as being a privilege and a duty of government employees when they see wrongdoing to turn it in. So I made no effort to find out who did this. Although

he never spoke to me directly about it, I was told indirectly that he was unhappy and felt that if I wanted to I could control . . . [employees who were going to the inspector general]. Somehow . . . [I was supposed to be able to] prevent the staff from parading his embarrassment by turning him in to the inspector general. My response was, I did nothing. Needless to say, there was a fair amount of tension between him and I.

Box 3.1 Résumé of a Government Guerrilla

1998–Present
Retired
Occasional adjunct professor

1992–1998
Special Assistant
Chair, Quality Improvement Board
U.S. Environmental Protection Agency
Washington, DC

1992–1998
Visiting Scholar, Indiana University
School of Public and Environmental Affairs
Bloomington, Indiana
Corecipient: Undergraduate Adjunct Faculty of the Year Award

1990–1992
Deputy Regional Administrator
U.S. Environmental Protection Agency
Chicago, Illinois
Recipient: Presidential Rank Award, Meritorious Executive 1991

1984–1990
Director, Environmental Services Division
U.S. Environmental Protection Agency
Seattle, Washington

1981–1984
Deputy Director, Environmental Services Division
U.S. Environmental Protection Agency
Seattle, Washington

(Continued)

Box 3.1 (Continued)

1980–1981
Director, Management Division
U.S. Environmental Protection Agency
Seattle, Washington

1979–1980
Chief, Resources Management Branch
U.S. Environmental Protection Agency
Seattle, Washington

1977–1979
Chief, Air Compliance Branch
U.S. Environmental Protection Agency
Seattle, Washington

1972–1977
Chief, Surveillance Branch
U.S. Environmental Protection Agency
Seattle, Washington

1971–1972
Microbiologist
U.S. Environmental Protection Agency
Seattle, Washington

1969–1971
Microbiologist
U.S. Department of the Interior
Portland, Oregon

1967–1969
Microbiologist
U.S. Department of the Interior
Pacific Northwest Water Laboratory
Corvallis, Oregon

1966–1967
Microbiologist
U.S. Department of the Interior
Vessel Pollution Study
San Diego, California

1964–1966
Microbiologist
U.S. Public Health Service
Division of Water Supply and Pollution Control
Atlanta, Georgia

1961–1964
Biological Sciences Assistant
U.S. Army Environmental Hygiene Agency
Edgewood Arsenal, Maryland

1960–1961
Junior Microbiologist
State of California Department of Public Health
Berkeley, California

When that same director of the Management Division, a man whose appointment to the Senior Executive Service was nearly complete prior to Spencer's arrival, repeatedly told Spencer that procedures needed to be followed and public funds could not be used for personal trips or for a personal driver, Spencer retaliated by transferring the director to a new position he had created for him in another division and refused to finalize his SES appointment:

> He called me into his office and told me that he wasn't comfortable in doing business with me and he wanted to reassign me. I asked him why. His answer was that he just was uncomfortable doing business with me. . . . [I was later told that he] wanted to make an example of one of his division directors to show the rest of his staff that he had the ability to fire somebody. I think that would be consistent with his "management by stark terror" idea. Show the staff that you have the ability and the will to remove somebody if they displease you.

From that day on, throughout Spencer's tenure, the former director of the Management Division was excluded from most senior management meetings.

Next, Spencer lobbied the Army Corps of Engineers, on behalf of a yacht club of which he was a member, for rapid approval of a dredging permit. Spencer mailed the yacht club's application to the corps, attaching a cover letter written on EPA stationary and signed by him as regional administrator, asking the corps to issue a permit the same week. He wrote a second letter the following month, emphasizing that "quick action is imperative" (UPI, March 9, 1983). The letters became part of the public record, and when environmentalists later discovered them, they quickly went to the press. The yacht club eventually withdrew the request and replaced it with another, which was denied because of concerns expressed by the Washington State Department of Game.

Spencer also was criticized for not enforcing the law as vigorously as possible. An example is the case of the Western Processing Company of Kent, Washington, which continually delayed the cleanup of hazardous waste (UPI, April 2, 1983). The EPA could have assessed penalties against the company of up to $5,000 per day for failure to implement an EPA cleanup order, but it did not. "For the time being," Spencer was quoted as saying, "with the promise of cooperation from Western Processing, EPA will forgo litigation" (BNA *Environment Reporter*, September 24, 1982), despite the fact that EPA officials said the chemicals at the site had the potential to threaten the city of Kent's water supplies (UPI, April 29, 1983).

Similarly, Spencer, whose nomination to the EPA post was shepherded by Senator Ted Stevens (R-Alaska), tentatively approved wastewater treatment exemptions for two large Alaska pulp mills during his tenure (UPI, November 29, 1984). According to EPA staff who analyzed the application, the exemptions clearly were not warranted under the law. The approval was eventually overturned by Spencer's successor, Ernesta Barnes.

In the same pulp mill case, Spencer ordered EPA staff to release confidential information provided by ITT-Rayonier, operator of pulp mills at Port Angeles and Hoquiam, to two of ITT-Rayonier's competitors (UPI, August 9, 1983). One former EPA employee described the situation:

> The engineer [who drafted the report containing confidential business information] took the report, as demanded [by Spencer] to the regional administrator . . . and the regional administrator wasn't in his office. He was gone for the day, and the engineer asked what to do with the report and he was instructed to give it to a person who was waiting in the regional administrator's office. When he went into the office he recognized the person as being associated with . . . [the competitor's] mill. . . . So the engineer . . . refused to give him the report.

The engineer went back to his office to discuss the matter with his colleagues. They decided to stamp the notice "Confidential Business Information" throughout the report, "so there would be no doubt about what parts of it legally were not disclosable," and then they hand delivered it to the regional administrator's home. The staff members suspected that Spencer gave the report to the competing mill anyway, but they waited to act on their suspicions.

Spencer's name also showed up in a report concerning alleged political uses of Superfund moneys by Susan Baldyga, a special assistant to fired EPA assistant administrator Rita Lavelle, who had forged "sweetheart deals" with industry and had lied to Congress. U.S. Representative Norm Dicks (D-Washington) publicly charged Spencer with participating in a plan allegedly fostered by the Reagan administration to use $1.6 billion of Superfund money "to help re-elect Republicans" (UPI, March 23, 1983). Spencer strongly denied the allegations, but he resigned as regional administrator less than two weeks later, soon after

Anne Gorsuch and eighteen other high-level EPA officials were fired or resigned.[2] Many of the Seattle EPA regional office staff vowed never again to tolerate a regional administrator like Spencer or to cooperate with a "reign of terror." The stage had been set for more extreme guerrilla government activity.

Gorsuch resigned under a cloud of controversy. She had slashed the EPA budget, destroyed morale at the agency, and alienated Congress by refusing to provide an investigation committee with documents concerning the agency's controversial Superfund program. Further, Gorsuch had targeted particular career EPA staff and advisory board members to be fired, hired, or promoted because of their political leanings. The Senior Executives Association (SEA) asked the Office of Special Counsel of the Merit Systems Protection Board to begin an investigation of these actions. Gorsuch's "hit list," which was released by a congressional committee investigating the activities at the EPA, included comments about individuals such as "bleeding heart liberal" and "invidious environmental extremist" (BNA *Environment Reporter,* April 7, 1983).

"This kind of abuse of the merit system represents a gross violation of the Civil Service Reform Act," said SEA president Jean Courturier in a press release. "If uncorrected, [it] would have a chilling effect on the career Senior Executive Service. . . . This type of political shenanigans threatens the very basis of the career merit system" (BNA *Environment Reporter,* April 7, 1983).

Spencer, the first of the Reagan-era regional administrators to resign, went to work for Riedel International, Inc., a firm involved in maritime construction, transportation, and environmental cleanup, as senior vice president. He quit his EPA job after only eighteen months. Before he left the EPA, Riedel International was awarded an EPA contract to clean up the hazardous Western Processing plant. The contract was not awarded in a competitive bidding process, said Jim Willman, chief of the EPA's Region 10 emergency response team, because cleanup at the Western site constituted an "emergency" (UPI, April 20, 1983).

The week Spencer announced his resignation, EPA career staff members went to the inspector general again. One described the situation:

> He [Spencer] came around to announce that he was going to leave. He had secured a job in private industry. So it really was that I had a dilemma in my mind at that point: Should I do anything about my suspicions that he had given confidential business information to this company or not? And after thinking about it for a period of time, I decided that I should call the Inspector General's Office and share my concerns with them.
>
> My reasons, to be candid with you, were that I really believed that this individual was not the kind of person to be in public service. I wanted to raise a cloud over his candidacy. Even though he was leaving, it was unlikely that anybody would do anything, but I wanted there to be something on the record that might indicate there was a question about his performance in the event that he was ever considered for public office again.

Spencer's actions were investigated by the EPA's Office of the Inspector General, in consultation with the Office of the U.S. Attorney General. In a report issued August 8, 1983, the investigators concluded that while Spencer engaged in improprieties, there was "insufficient evidence to warrant criminal action" (U.S. Environmental Protection Agency 1983). On August 9, 1983, UPI reported that "Paul E. Olson, EPA's assistant inspector general, said prosecution wasn't warranted because no harm was done—[there was insufficient evidence to conclude that] the confidential information was . . . released and the marina never got the dredging permit." EPA career staff were stunned and disappointed at the mild report from the Inspector General's Office.

EPA staff had been taken aback by Spencer. Never before had they had a regional administrator with whom they clashed so much. One EPA employee put it this way:

> The whole organization, I think, was surprised by the degree to which they had been traumatized by this guy. Morale was pretty bad, fear was among people, and the trust level was practically zero. I think that under his [Spencer's] administration not many of the staff trusted him . . . and those who cooperated with him, I think their credibility . . . had been severely damaged.

As a new regional administrator was about to be appointed, EPA Region 10 staff geared up for a fight. They had learned from their negative dealings with Spencer and felt they had been too easy on him. Those who had confronted Spencer directly had been reassigned or demoted. Those who had appealed to the next person in the chain of command had been placed on Gorsuch's hit list. Some no longer trusted the Inspector General's Office. Staff initially were hesitant to leak information to the press, viewing such action as unprofessional. It was better to resolve things internally, they thought. As a result of the Spencer experience, however, EPA Region 10 staff members became more open to guerrilla activities, including leaking information to the press.

They braced themselves for more intense battles and informally talked about how to survive the next regional administrator through more intensive "guerrilla warfare." One guerrilla phrased his ambivalence in this way:

> [The situation] created a dilemma I think on the part of the public servant. You are there to serve the R.A. [regional administrator]—you are there to serve the political appointee—and so forming these [guerrilla government] coalitions or whatever you want to call it—to resist what you perceive to be improper decisions or improper behavior—you are really treading on a very fine line there.

Many EPA staff concluded that one course of action available to them was to not protect political appointees. "Let them go forward and suffer the consequences," said one staff member. "Let them make some dumb decision and maybe that will shorten their careers." To the staff members' surprise, however, no such tactics were needed—at least for the next three years.

ERNESTA BARNES, 1983–1986:
GUERRILLA ACTIVITY WANES

On June 8, 1983, Seattle banker Ernesta Barnes was appointed the next administrator of the Seattle regional office by newly appointed returning EPA administrator William Ruckelshaus. She said that the appointment was a "great honor" and emphasized that her skill was working with people (UPI, June 8, 1983). Environmentalists were "wary" (UPI, June 8, 1983). Prior to working at the Seattle Trust and Savings Bank, Barnes was director of public service for the Municipality of Metropolitan Seattle (METRO), which operates the county transit system and manages water quality for Seattle. Before that, Barnes was director of the budget for the University of Washington and founder of the Sound Savings and Loan Association, a business owned and organized by women.

Ruckelshaus announced that he and his regional administrators would foster an "open process" with the public and would act "in the public interest" (UPI, June 9, 1983). Barnes herself announced that she would act as "vigorous[ly] as the existing laws allow" (UPI, June 8, 1983). By most accounts Barnes did just that, establishing herself as a model regional administrator. One of her first highly symbolic and savvy actions was to promote the former director of the Management Division who had been fired by Spencer to the position of deputy regional administrator. This action immediately won her the approval of career EPA employees. The new deputy regional administrator described his view of his promotion:

> And low and behold she selected me for the job [of deputy regional administrator]. I'm not certain why, but I think one of the reasons may have been that she felt that I had integrity in the way I handled the situation with the former regional administrator and I had credibility with the staff. So I wound up one station higher in the organization than I had ever aspired to before.

Barnes served as regional administrator for three years. Among the items that stand out in her record of service are her successes in increasing the number of EPA staff in areas of critical concern in the Northwest (UPI, December 13, 1984) and in greatly improving morale in the agency. She never hesitated to defend EPA staff when she thought they were right, maintaining—often under fire—that they acted "firmly and responsibly in correcting problems" (UPI, August 23, 1984). She reversed John Spencer's previous approval of wastewater treatment exemptions for the two Alaska pulp mills (UPI, September 19, 1984).[3] She campaigned vigorously to make the American people realize the economic impact of pollution (UPI, August 11, 1984),[4] penalized local governments that failed to follow environmental laws (UPI, August 15, 1983; September 19, 1983; July 25, 1984; September 5, 1984; September 12, 1984; February 22, 1985), and did not hesitate to criticize inadequate state pollution programs (BNA *Environment Reporter*, October 21, 1983).

Barnes fostered a get-tough policy on cleaning up Puget Sound, cracking down on nonpoint sources of pollution (BNA *Environment Reporter*, August 23, 1985), forcing sewage treatment plants to upgrade, and denying requests for waivers of pollution laws (UPI, August 8, 1984). She declared, "How can anyone not want to clean up Puget Sound?" (Turner 1984) and "I don't feel awkward about defending the Clean Water Act" (Stanfield 1985). She forged alliances with the U.S. Attorney's Office in order to strengthen EPA enforcement efforts (Green 1985), forged alliances with states to regulate federal government polluters (UPI, February 6, 1986),[5] and boasted that her office had "embraced the law" (BNA *Environment Reporter*, November 1, 1985). She forced a settlement of the Western Processing plant problem that her predecessor had failed to address (UPI, June 19, 1984). She reprimanded the U.S. Department of Defense for its mishandling of a shipment of transformers containing PCBs (polychlorinated biphenyls) (UPI, March 15, 1984) and barred contractors who failed to comply with wage agreements from participating in projects funded by the EPA (UPI, January 16, 1984). Barnes, together with Ruckelshaus, launched an enormous public participation program to help determine whether the ASARCO plant in Tacoma should be shut down because of arsenic emissions (Kalikow 1984; Barringer 1983; UPI, September 9, 1983). One reporter wrote: "At the EPA, Regional Administrator Ernesta Barnes is given credit for pushing the agency past a time when it relied on a conciliatory attitude toward business—'take a polluter to lunch,' as environmentalists dubbed it" (UPI, March 31, 1985).

Barnes stepped down as Region 10 administrator in March 1986 and became the president and chief executive officer of Pacific Celebration '89, a not-for-profit corporation created by Washington State to promote trade, tourism, and cultural exchange during the state's centennial year of 1989. When she left the EPA, newspapers called her "highly respected" (UPI, November 29, 1984). One leader of Friends of the Earth, an environmental organization, reported, "She's been fair and we've had access to her" (UPI, November 29, 1984). When Barnes's deputy administrator was named acting regional administrator upon Barnes's resignation, guerrilla activity was largely nonexistent in the EPA's Seattle regional office.

ROBIE RUSSELL, 1986–1990: GUERRILLA GOVERNMENT IS TRIGGERED AGAIN

On June 17, 1986, Robie Russell, a senior deputy attorney general from Idaho, was named to succeed Ernesta Barnes, and guerrilla government emerged once again in the EPA Region 10 office. Russell previously had held the position of acting chief of the Natural Resources Division at the attorney general's office, where he had responsibilities for public lands, water resources, environmental protection, parks and recreation, fish and game, and agricultural issues. A former Republican Party county chairman, he also had worked as an attorney at the law firm of Bielenberg, Anderson and Walker in Moscow, Idaho.

By all accounts, Robie Russell's tenure at the EPA started out like Ernesta Barnes's tenure. While there was some skepticism among EPA staff and the regulated industries, most were supportive of him. His earliest press releases seemed to echo Barnes's sentiments. He talked about the "fine staff of dedicated people" at Region 10 and his preferred "management [style of] . . . example and consensus." "When people are reaching their objectives they should have the opportunity to participate," Russell said. The new administrator also said that he would not hesitate to use enforcement when necessary and expressed support for the new civil investigator the regional office had just hired. "In the broadest sense of the word I'm an environmentalist," he quipped (Gilbreath 1986).

Russell's early actions as administrator also were reminiscent of actions taken by Barnes. In a strongly worded letter he warned a local pollution authority that it could lose federal money if it did not strengthen its approach to controlling toxics discharged into Puget Sound (UPI, November 4, 1986). He filed legal action against nine companies accused of violating Superfund laws, warning them that they could not "simply walk away from the mess they helped create" (UPI, November 21, 1986). He urged states in the Northwest to forge a pact to deal with common hazardous waste challenges, chastising those who held NIMBY (not in my backyard) attitudes (Flash 1987) and inviting them to a regional conference to discuss hazardous waste issues with local governments, industry representatives, and environmentalists from Washington, Oregon, Idaho, and Alaska (UPI, April 23, 1987).

By the end of March 1987 (less than a year into his term as regional administer), however, Russell's honeymoon was over. Local media announced that a "veteran" engineer had quit his EPA job in anger, a disgusted branch chief was seeking to be "loaned" to another agency, and a resentful section supervisor had been involuntarily transferred to a different job (UPI, March 23, 1987). All alleged that Russell had taken too soft a stance on two important cases: one involving proposed oil drilling in the Arctic National Wildlife Refuge and one involving dredging in the U.S. Navy port in Everett, Washington.

Russell began making his most important decisions in closed-door meetings with only his division heads present. Most of the time he did not even include his deputy administrator—the same career administrator who had served as deputy under Ernesta Barnes. The deputy responded by holding a series of clandestine guerrilla government–style meetings with the division directors prior to their meetings with Russell. The group would agree on unified staff recommendations and then present these to Russell in the closed-door meetings. The deputy described the process as follows:

> I wasn't invited to come to the meetings. . . . So the way we dealt with that was I would meet privately with the division directors before their meeting with the R.A. and they would brief me on the issue and I would tell my feelings about the issue and expect them to articulate a staff position. . . . That's how I kept my oar in the water. We would often discuss what we needed to do in order to try to steer the R.A. back on a path that we felt . . . we were most comfortable with.

I felt pretty awkward in this situation, almost like I was being kind of conniving with the division directors in plotting a strategy behind his back.

Staff members were also concerned that some who had performed the analyses forwarded to the administrator had been cut out of the decision-making process by Russell, that Russell was deleting negative comments in reports before the reports were released to the public, and that those who dared to question the administrator were being ostracized. A UPI report quoted Russell's response to these allegations:

> The only difference is I've asked the division directors to get in there and be involved, rather than dealing on every issue direct. There haven't been any big dramatic changes in the agency. I'll never be Ernesta. I should be measured by my own performance. My management style isn't inconsistent with the way the agency is set up. What the hell is the problem? There is no problem. You have people who have gotten used to doing things in a certain way, and now it's being done differently. (UPI, March 23, 1987)

Some EPA staff concluded that all-out guerrilla warfare was inevitable.

After publicly blasting an environmental impact statement from the U.S. Department of the Interior for not adequately analyzing possible negative effects on wildlife and the environment of a proposed oil development in the Arctic National Wildlife Refuge (UPI, June 12, 1987; *Inside Energy*, June 15, 1987), Russell abruptly backed off and gave his support to the project (Dolan 1987). In June 1987, Russell had announced that an EPA analysis concluded that the DOI document was "incomplete in its presentation of scientific data" and did not adequately address the majority of the EPA's concerns in the areas of air quality impacts, demands on freshwater supplies, and effects on marine fish populations (*Inside Energy*, June 15, 1987). One month later, in July 1987, Russell seemed to reverse himself when he testified before a U.S. House of Representatives panel considering the proposal that the "EPA does not oppose the environmentally acceptable development of the Arctic National Wildlife Refuge" (Dolan 1987; Woutat 1987). The action infuriated both environmentalists and the EPA staff members who had worked on the EPA analysis.

In November 1987, Russell was blasted by the press, who had been tipped off by an EPA staff member, for spending too much time in his home state of Idaho. One news account concluded:

> EPA records show that so far this year Robie G. Russell has spent all or part of 43 days on official travel in Idaho, three times the 13 days he has spent on official travel in Oregon, Alaska, and in Washington outside the EPA's regional office in Seattle. (UPI, November 3, 1987)

Russell shrugged off the criticism, explaining that he was "more in tune" with Idaho environmental issues and had been asked to the state more often than the other states in his region. When accused of using government moneys to fund private trips to Idaho, Russell said he "occasionally" mixed business with pleasure, but such actions were minor, such as having lunch with friends. One press report concluded that eight of Russell's official trips to Idaho included weekends or vacation time. The same report quoted an environmentalist attorney in Idaho as saying, "I can say this: His travel back to Idaho hasn't produced any great results with the environment" (UPI, November 3, 1987). EPA staff went back to the inspector general.

In July 1988 the EPA Inspector General's Office released a twenty-seven-page report on an investigation into Russell's travel habits, which stated that no evidence of criminal or administrative wrongdoing had been found. The Inspector General's Office determined that while Russell made sixteen trips to Idaho between July 10, 1986, and September 26, 1987, and twelve of those trips involved weekends off, Russell did not charge any personal expenses to the government. "Russell [as the agency's 'approving official'] was in a position to arrange his own travel schedule and if he made personal as well as official contacts on his own time during these trips, that was his affair," the report concluded (U.S. Environmental Protection Agency 1988). Again, some EPA staff were stunned and disappointed.

In March 1989, Russell had refused to make public a draft EPA analysis concluding that Idaho potatoes may pose a health risk because the pesticide aldicarb is used on them. An EPA guerrilla leaked the information to the press, and upset citizens contacted the White House, the EPA, and state health and environment officials. Grocery stores around the world pulled potatoes from their shelves. Russell responded by making public a letter he had written to Governor Cecil Andrus of Idaho, in which Russell indicated that he shared the governor's irritation about the unauthorized leak, emphasizing that there was not enough scientific evidence to conclude a negative health effect stemming from the ingestion of potatoes that had been treated with the pesticide (UPI, March 31, 1989).

In June 1989, Russell was reappointed by new EPA administrator William Reilly after George H. W. Bush became president of the United States. Within weeks, EPA employees sent Reilly the results of a self-initiated in-house survey that slammed Russell. In addition, environmentalists from three states followed suit by sending Reilly a letter calling for Russell's ouster. The environmentalists' letter, which received wide press coverage in the northwest United States, was signed by the Sierra Club, Friends of the Earth, the Oregon Natural Resources Council, the Washington Toxics Coalition, the Alaska Center for the Environment, and the Northern Alaska Environmental Center. Fueled by data supplied by EPA guerrillas, the letter fired off specific accusations: Russell spent three times as many days in Idaho as he did in other states in the region, he supported the navy's 1987 decision to dispose of toxic dredge spoils in Puget Sound, and he approved the filling of a wetland in Warrenton, Oregon, for a shopping mall over the objections of EPA staff. Further, he approved less stringent water pollution discharge emission limitations than those recommended by EPA staff for four sites in Washington State—Fort Lewis, Bangor, McChord Air Force Base, and Hanford—three of which had experienced groundwater contamination as a result of the administrator's decision (UPI, August 15, 1989).

In response to the criticism, Russell issued a defensive press release pointing out that he had the full support of William Reilly, the administrator of the EPA. Further, he emphasized that he had tried to "bring balance" to the administration of environmental laws and regulations. At the same time he acknowledged his critics, saying:

> I can see where some environmentalists might not care for my record. I can understand where some businessmen might not care for my record. And, there may be people within my own agency who also don't agree with the course that I have followed. (UPI, August 15, 1989)

On January 29, 1990, after three and a half years in the Seattle EPA office, Robie Russell announced that he was resigning as regional administrator to consider a run for the U.S. Senate or for the position of attorney general of Idaho. (In fact he ended up doing neither; he joined a Seattle law firm.) Many speculated that the real reason for Russell's resignation was the retirement of his "godfather," Senator James McClure of Idaho. EPA career staff held parties to celebrate.

Additional audits by the Inspector General's Office were under way, prompted by complaints from EPA guerrillas, and according to one newspaper article, EPA "employees . . . lined up outside the audit team's door to provide it with information" (Dietrich 1990a). Complaints ranged from caustic allegations that Russell purchased photos with EPA funds after he had announced his resignation to sharp allegations that Russell or one of his immediate employees asked a local hotel to disguise food and bartender bills paid for with EPA funds as room rental (Wilson 1990)[6] to devastating allegations that Russell had promoted violations of environmental laws. One newspaper summed up their concerns:

> Some EPA employees complained Russell failed to back tough enforcement, sabotaged cleanup efforts that would have hurt industry in his native Idaho and was the target of a still-unreleased audit critical of his performance. . . . Employees lobbied [William] Reilly last year to replace Russell, starting an in-house survey with generally blistering comments about their boss, some of which were mailed to the [Seattle] Times. . . . "It has nothing to do with the fact he was a Reagan appointee," one employee said commenting on staff unhappiness. "Reagan appointed Ernesta Barnes before Robie and she was an excellent administrator. We just felt there was a lack of objective decision-making in the agency." (Wilson 1990)

Russell again defended his record by maintaining that he brought "badly needed balance" to the EPA. Environmentalists maintained that he had "stifled a lot of good effort and energy that . . . [had] been coming up from his staff" and vowed to seek a replacement who "has a commitment to environmental preservation" (Wilson 1990).

After Russell announced his resignation, the Inspector General's Office issued two additional reports on his actions while he was Region 10 administrator. The first report gave him a symbolic slap on the wrist by charging him $110 for photographs of himself ordered after he had announced his resignation. The report also supported staff allegations that Russell or one of his immediate employees asked a local hotel to disguise food and bartender bills paid for with EPA funds as room rental. Concerned senior EPA staff took up a collection and paid the $311 bill (U.S. Environmental Protection Agency 1990a).

The second report was more scathing. It concluded that Russell had improperly blocked his own staff's efforts to clean up a Superfund site in his home state of Idaho. A summary of the report stated:

> As a result, the smelter complex was allowed to deteriorate to the point that it was declared a public health hazard, . . . prompt action was not taken to protect the public from contamination resulting from salvage operations, and partners in the Bunker Limited Partnership moved company assets to other corporations through stock and property transfers, which is expected to complicate attempts to recover cleanup costs. (Dietrich 1990b)

Among other consequences, railroad ties covered with lead dust were sold throughout the Spokane area to nurseries for use in landscaping. Worse, eight years after the smelter was closed, 8 of every 275 children in the area still had unsafe levels of lead in their blood. (Lead poisoning causes nerve and blood disorders that can affect IQ and even cause death at times.) The *Seattle Times* concluded: "The blistering audit is the first official confirmation of EPA employee complaints that Russell discouraged enforcement of pollution regulations in his native Idaho" (Dietrich 1990b). Further, the inspector general wrote in the summary accompanying the report, "Nearly every Region 10 employee who we interviewed about the Bunker Hill site expressed fear of retaliation [from Russell]" (U.S. Environmental Protection Agency 1990b).

The EPA guerrillas were ecstatic. Their guerrilla government activities had paid off. They had successfully stemmed the reign of terror started years earlier by John Spencer. Future regional administrators would know that they were a force to be reckoned with.

A division director who had collaborated with guerrillas in the Russell case and had been punished by Russell with a poor performance appraisal was treated differently after Russell's departure. EPA career managers who knew the real story saw to it that he received a superior performance bonus in a subsequent appraisal cycle. He ultimately became the deputy regional administrator for Region 10.

EPILOGUE

I recently received this interesting correspondence from one of the guerrillas in the EPA Seattle regional office, who, after twenty-three years of reflection, has this to say about guerrilla government:

> There is another dimension to my story which you may want to explore further. In my case engaging in guerrilla government exacted a personal cost to my self-esteem which nags at me to this day. Some people engaging in guerrilla

government may feel self-righteous. That certainly wasn't my feeling at the time or now. I was taught to value loyalty and straightforwardness and therefore didn't like myself for what I was doing. Nevertheless, I abandoned these values temporarily because I saw a necessary greater good to be served. The point is, people who may be contemplating engaging in guerrilla government should know how it might affect them emotionally. Perhaps not uplifting. This translates into an interesting question: How do people who were engaging in guerrilla government feel emotionally at the time about their sub-rosa activities, and how do they feel now? In my case I'm still conflicted.

NOTES

1. All quotes are from 1995 interviews unless otherwise noted.

2. In addition to Gorsuch and Spencer, from February 1 through May 21, 1983, the following EPA political appointees resigned or were fired: Rita Lavelle, assistant administrator for solid waste and emergency response; Warren Wood, aide to Lavelle; Susan Baldyga, aide to Lavelle; Eugene Ingold, aide to Lavelle; John Horton, assistant administrator for administration; Mathew Novick, inspector general; John Hernandez, deputy administrator, acting administrator; Robert Perry, general counsel; John Todhunter, assistant administrator for pesticides and toxic substances; Paul Cahill, director, Office of Federal Activities; John Daniel, chief of staff; Steve Durham, administrator, Denver regional office; Richard Funkhouser, director, Office of International Activities; Frederic Eidsness Jr., assistant administrator for water; Kathleen Bennett, assistant administrator, air, noise, and radiation; Peter Bibko, administrator, Philadelphia regional office; Lester Sutton, administrator, Boston regional office; Michael Sawyer, aide to administrator, Office of International Activities.

3. The two mills were Alaska Pulp Corporation in Sitka and Louisiana Pacific in Ketchikan.

4. Barnes said publicly in many speeches: "We have been led to assume that the basic costs of living are low. It's going to be a hard lesson . . . for a lot of Americans to learn that it costs a lot to dispose of our garbage [and] to address our pollution problems."

5. Perhaps the best example is her ordering of joint action with the state of Washington against the U.S. Department of Energy's Hanford site for violations of hazardous waste laws (UPI, February 6, 1986).

6. Russell also was charged with reckless driving after he allegedly tried to run down two University of Idaho students working as traffic controllers who refused him access to a VIP parking lot at a university basketball game. (Russell was the national president of the University of Idaho Boosters Club at the time.)

Second Interlude:
More Stories of Guerrilla
Government

STORIES OF GUERRILLA GOVERNMENT are rarely reported, primarily because many guerrillas do not want to talk about their activities. There are a few stories, however, circulating in classroom case studies. Here are some of the most interesting.

GUERRILLA GOVERNMENT
IN COUNTY PLANNING

Gwen Lewis was director of the Planning Department of St. Claire County, Washington.[1] In the mid-1990s, a battle broke out concerning which areas of the county would be developed and which would be preserved in the county's long-term plan. Lewis's boss, county council chair Victor Long, first approved the planning staff's idea of freezing growth pending a more comprehensive professional analysis, but then he began to change his mind after being heavily lobbied and as his reelection campaign seemed threatened. What bothered Lewis the most about her boss's change of mind was her fear that it signaled a departure from professional growth management practices and a return to the old days of caving in to the demands of powerful land developers who contribute generously to the campaigns of the county legislators.

In the tug-of-war that ensued between some county elected officials and the professional staff, Lewis was told to stay out of the fight and not to present her professional opinion, or the professional opinions of her staff, at public meetings. Later the staff members were told not to attempt to influence the final vote in any manner. Long chastised Lewis: "Gwen, I'm telling you in the clearest language possible, I do not want you or any member of your staff to lift even a finger to influence the outcome when the full council votes on the interim . . . [plan]. . . . If

I hear that any of you were involved, that's it. You're fired. . . . And Frank and Jean [Lewis's chief staff members] will be too" (Brock 1998, B1).

After a brief period of soul-searching, Lewis and her two chief staff members became government guerrillas. In the name of good government and professional planning, they clandestinely plotted a strategy to influence the outcome of the vote, hoping that the final tally would support their recommendation that the plan be frozen pending a more sophisticated long-range analysis. Their strategy included drafting and liberally distributing fact sheets for potential supporters; making lists of possible allies from a wide array of interest groups, then contacting them and asking them to either write letters or make phone calls of support; meeting with members of the editorial boards of the four local newspapers to encourage them to publish positive editorials; and asking the local president of the League of Women Voters to request more public testimony, then lining up more than 150 people to testify in favor of the staff's recommendation.

In response to the guerrillas' efforts, the council received more than 300 phone calls and 175 letters in favor of the staff's position. On the day of the final vote, 178 people testified, 90 percent of them in favor of the staff proposal. The final vote was six to three in favor of the staff's recommendation. Amazingly, Lewis's boss never found out about her actions and in the end was thrilled with the positive media coverage he received for his initial support of the staff recommendation (Brock, 1998).

GUERRILLA GOVERNMENT
IN THE LEGAL SERVICES ORGANIZATION

David Goldman was a young lawyer and community organizer who worked for the federally funded Legal Services Organization (LSO). The LSO's lawyers were explicitly forbidden by federal statute from representing any labor union, from organizing clients into collective bargaining units, and from holding other legal jobs. For most of his time as an LSO attorney, Goldman technically did not disobey the letter of the law, although he devoted most of his energy to behaving in a way that was contrary to the law's intent. An admirer of Cesar Chavez and a supporter of Chavez's new farmworkers' union, Goldman continually reminded his staff that the union was their "real" client and that they should keep that in mind when making all major decisions. Goldman was a government guerrilla who worked quietly to support the farmworkers' union against the wishes of his superiors and against congressional mandate.

On one occasion Chavez asked Goldman a legal question about a potential boycott. Goldman and his staff stayed up all night working on the answer. When word leaked out to the press and the White House that LSO attorneys were giving Chavez legal advice, a White House aide telephoned Goldman. "We don't have any problems with that, do we?" the aide asked. "None," Goldman answered, and the matter was dropped (Hitchner 1994, 7).

GUERRILLA GOVERNMENT IN JOB CORPS

William P. Kelly was the director of Job Corps, a federal program in the Office of Economic Opportunity. Within six months of inheriting the poorly managed and beleaguered program, Kelly had masterfully expanded it, instituted performance measurement, improved the program's public relations, hired pollster Lou Harris to survey participants to convince skeptics that Job Corps was worth fighting for, and built a power base among his staff, the White House, and Congress.

Kelly began his guerrilla government activities when he became aware that memos he was sending to the president were apparently not reaching him. Kelly arranged to have a letter appealing a $50 million Bureau of the Budget cut for Job Corps slipped into the president's night reading folder. The president was convinced, and he intervened and saved the $50 million from being shifted away from Job Corps.

When a new presidential administration began efforts to abolish Job Corps, Kelly ratcheted up his guerrilla government activities. He clandestinely fed questions to members of congressional committees to ask of those who testified against retaining Job Corps. The questions were so tough that any challengers, including Secretary of Labor George Shultz, looked like idiots and were embarrassed publicly. Kelly also lobbied the media: stories emerged in major newspapers and magazines praising Job Corps and criticizing the president for trying to abolish the program. When a delegation from the Department of Labor visited Kelly's office and asked him which Job Corps centers, if closed, would have the most political impact in Congress, Kelly told the political appointees:

> If you guys are so bright you figure it out. I'm not going to tell you a damn thing. I'm not even going to tell you whose district they're in—*you* look it up. *You* figure it out. Don't come over here and tell me that you want me to participate in making political decisions about closing down this program because I'm not going to do it. Go away. (Ridout 1974, 13)

GUERRILLA GOVERNMENT IN THE DEPARTMENT OF LABOR

In 1980, Raymond Donovan was confirmed as the U.S. secretary of labor. Al Zuck, a veteran civil servant of twenty-three years, was acting secretary of the department prior to Donovan's confirmation and then returned to his post of assistant secretary for administration and management within the department. As one of his first acts in office, Donovan requested that Zuck award a sole-source contract for $500,000 to the person who successfully ran the media campaign for the Reagan/Bush 1980 election campaign. That person was starting his own consulting firm and had asked Donovan if he could do a study of the department's public relations and information activities. Donovan said yes and ordered Zuck to award the sole-source contract.

Zuck refused to issue the contract for several reasons. First, it would be politically embarrassing to the secretary when it became public knowledge that that one of his first acts was to award a large contract to a former political colleague. Second, none of the reasons for a sole-source contact, such as urgency or national security, existed. Third, awarding the contract as he had been ordered to do didn't pass what Zuck called the "smell" test. Even though there most likely would be some lawyer somewhere who would sign off on the contract, at a minimum awarding it to Donovan's former colleague would have the appearance of impropriety. In Zuck's eyes, it was an issue of ethics, public policy, and public perception.

For several weeks, Donovan pressured Zuck directly and indirectly to issue the contract. At one point, Donovan said to Zuck: "You know you are just the stereotype of the career bureaucrat. Don't you realize that there was an election? There was a mandate from the people. You are just an obstacle to achieving that mandate. Fellow, you had better shape up, or you are going to ship out" (Gortner 2000, 3).

Despite the fact that Donovan never understood the ethical principle that Zuck was articulating, Zuck stood firm. The secretary did, however, finally grasp that Zuck was trying to protect him. By the end of his term, Zuck felt that the secretary understood that Zuck had done him a favor. Zuck reflected on his experience:

> At the point at which I left the Department in 1983 [to retire], . . . [Donovan] said that I, more than any of his other immediate staff, was objective and had his interest at heart. I believe that to be his honest opinion. I saw the issue as an ethical question in the broader definition of the public interest and the responsibility of public officials to proceed in a way that does not bring personal advantage or benefit in the performance of the public business. . . . I wanted to stake out a posture of political neutrality and ethical behavior. . . . I knew full well it could mean my head. . . . I [also] was trying, at the beginning of an administration with Donovan that I knew was going to be difficult, to stake out a position and let them know that I wasn't going to be pushed around in these kinds of issues. . . . Ultimately, the best advice for individuals facing similar ethical dilemmas is to really "call it as you see it." . . . Don't play "Mickey Mouse" games. The issue is ethics, not legality, in most cases, and the kind of behavior one should expect from those who occupy positions of public trust. (Gortner 2000, 5–7)

I followed up with Al Zuck in June 2005 via e-mail and asked him about his actions with the Donovan administration. With his permission, here are excerpts from our exchange.

June 18, 2005

Hello, Al—

. . . My book, tentatively entitled *Guerrilla Government,* is about career public servants who clandestinely take actions against the will of their superiors in order to "do the right thing." Such guerrilla activity was a possibility for you when you were at the Department of Labor. You could have leaked information to the press, given information clandestinely to interest groups, talked to a congressional staffer, gone above the secretary's head, gone to the IG, directly and openly blasted the secretary, asked for a transfer to another office/organization, quit, or taken other numerous actions. Yet you chose to "speak truth to power."

Why please?

Thanks,

Rosemary

June 19, 2005

Rosemary,

You pose an interesting question. As I reflect on it, it seems to me it would have been premature to take any such action. First, Donovan was brand new to the position and had no understanding of the culture of public service and I saw it as part of my responsibility to educate him to the importance of understanding the public nature of public service and how his action would have been perceived. Second, if I had gone public or brought external pressure, it would have colored his already dim view of the career service and would have been counterproductive. I wanted to have him understand that it was my job to give him my best professional advice and part of my responsibility was to protect him from the political realities of Washington. Third, I think it inevitably would have blown up in his face if the contract had been awarded. He was under a lot of scrutiny from the press as a result of his confirmation difficulties and a sole-source award would have had to be reported in the *Commerce Business Daily* and it would have become public information. Thus, no covert action would have been necessary.

Hope this helps.

Best regards,

Al

NOTE

1. The names and other identifiers in this case have been changed to protect the anonymity of the guerrillas.

Chapter

4

A Government Guerrilla
Sues His Own Agency:
Off-Road Vehicles in the
Hoosier National Forest

THIS STORY CONCERNS THE EFFORTS of a career employee of the U.S. Forest Service to protest and eventually halt the building of off-road vehicle trails in the Hoosier National Forest in Indiana. This story is about one man, Claude Ferguson, who "met the test of his lifetime" and, deviating from Forest Service norms, became a government guerrilla against the organization he loved.[1]

Claude Ferguson's website is hardly the manifestation of a radical environmentalist.[2] The site makes no mention of Earth First!, contains no statements about overthrowing the Forest Service, and gives no indication that Ferguson is anything other than a retired federal government employee living the simple life in the small town of Bedford, Indiana. Titled "You, Too, Can Play the Spoons," the website provides advice (while serenading the viewer with country music) concerning choice of spoons, body position, "hitting the beat and adding the off beat," and "adding variety or showing off." It includes a photo—once printed in the local newspaper—of Ferguson playing the spoons in bib overalls.

One would never know from his website that Claude Ferguson once worked with environmental groups to protest off-road vehicle (ORV) trails built in the Hoosier National Forest (HNF). One would never know that he joined in a lawsuit sponsored by environmentalists against his employer, the U.S. Forest Service. Nor would one know that as a government guerrilla Ferguson was the subject of an investigative report written by the U.S. Department of Agriculture.

Claude Ferguson first joined the U.S. Forest Service in 1940 as a lookout in the Mark Twain National Forest (MTNF) in Missouri while a senior in high school. He later served as a National Youth Administration crew member before his permanent appointment as a fire control aide with the Forest Service in the

MTNF. He worked closely with the Civilian Conservation Corps in fire control from three of that program's camps.

After three years in the U.S. Navy as an aviation radio-radar operator, gunner, and instructor during World War II, Ferguson returned to the MTNF as a forestry aide for four years, during which time he was engaged in timber management and land acquisition. Prior to working in the Hoosier National Forest, he worked as a forester in the Nicolet National Forest in Wisconsin, as district ranger in the Shawnee National Forest in Illinois, as district ranger in the Hiawatha National Forest in Upper Michigan, and as staff forester in the Ottawa National Forest in Upper Michigan in charge of lands, recreation, wildlife, soil, and water. He later served as chief of the Branch of Cooperative Forestry Management and chief of the Branch of Operations in the U.S. Forest Service's regional office in Milwaukee. In 1966, he was transferred to Bedford, Indiana, where he was forest supervisor for both the Hoosier National Forest in Indiana and the Wayne National Forest in Ohio. In 1971, he stepped down from the position of forest supervisor at his own request after he married another Forest Service employee. His successor was a man named Donald Girton, who will return later in this story.

Ferguson's awareness of an off-road vehicle problem in Indiana was sparked by an event that occurred in April 1970, when he was forest supervisor. The event was known as the Buffalo 100, named for John Buffalo, an avid motorcyclist who purchased twenty acres of private land located in the middle of the HNF. Without asking for permission or notifying the Forest Service, Buffalo and his associates marked a 100-mile trail through the forest and held a motorcycle race on the federal land. With the district ranger, Ferguson filmed the damage caused by the motorcyclists, including torn-up hiking trails, spoiled fragile forestland not meant for trails, trampled young trees, broken branches, destruction of wildlife habitat for both endangered and nonendangered species, littering, and excessive noise levels. In addition, several of the motorcyclists had sustained injuries such as fractured bones when their ORVs hit tree stumps and tree limbs.

When Ferguson told the organizers of the race the next year that they could not hold their event again in the national forest, they warned him that they "know how to strike matches," a not-too-veiled threat that they were willing to burn down portions of the forest if Ferguson did not kowtow to their demands. Ferguson told them to go talk to the Bureau of Motor Vehicles, as that is the agency that handles motorized vehicles. His job, Ferguson told them, was to protect the national forest.

In 1970, Ferguson presented a paper on the ORV challenge facing national parks in the United States at two conferences: the 24th Great Lakes Park Training Institute in February 1970 and the 20th Annual Great Lakes District Conference of the National Recreation and Park Association in April 1970. The bulk of his paper documented the damage done by ORV users in the Hoosier National

Forest. He later publicly agreed with Dr. Diana Dunn (1970), director of research for the National Recreation and Park Association, that it was no longer tolerable for forest supervisors to fail to manage ORVs, as most "ecocatastrophies" involving such vehicles resulted from nonactions and nondecisions by forest supervisors.

In March 1970, an interim ORV policy was adopted for the HNF that allowed limited use of the vehicles in a small number of approved areas. This development yielded an intensified study of the problem statewide. In April 1971, the Indiana General Assembly enacted legislation mandating the registration and regulation of off-road vehicles and their use, triggered by State Senator Earl Wilson's returning home one day to find dozens of motorcyclists riding on his private land without his permission. On October 8, 1971, the regional forester closed the HNF to ORV use pending the results of formal studies undertaken by the Forest Service and others. In February 1972, President Richard Nixon issued an executive order titled "Use of Off-Road Vehicles on Public Lands," which directed that the use of ORVs on public lands be controlled so as to protect the resources of those lands, to promote the safety of all users of those lands, and to minimize conflicts among the various users of those lands.

In September 1972, the Forest Service announced that, in accordance with the National Environmental Policy Act, a formal environmental impact statement would be written analyzing the ORV situation. In response, the employees of the HNF stepped up their data gathering and had many debates in staff meetings about the ORV situation. The employees were unanimous in their opposition to ORV use within the limited and fragile public lands of the forest.

The eastern national forests were established under the 1911 Weeks Act after public outcry concerning uncontrolled logging and fires. The act allowed the federal government to purchase private land east of the Mississippi River for the protection of the headwaters of navigable streams and for the production of timber. The boundaries of the Hoosier National Forest were drawn to embrace the lands of the Norman and Crawford physiographic regions in Indiana most susceptible to erosion by water. By definition, according to Ferguson, they would be the last soil types that should be selected for ORV use in Indiana.

"At every staff meeting I attended," Ferguson said, "there was not one staff member who supported the use of HNF lands for ORVs." He continued:

> After one of the many shows of hands on this question at a staff meeting, I questioned further consideration of the issue because we had reached a consensus. Mr. Girton, the forest supervisor, advised the group that this was an "erroneous consensus," and that he was speaking to a wealth of interdisciplinary professional people whom he had hired to counsel and advise him in their fields of expertise. Girton obviously felt he had to be all things to all people and that it was in our best interests to broaden our base of support beyond hikers, hunters, conservationists, and environmentalists. After several such meetings it became clear that the final ORV policy as adopted and implemented would be

solely Girton's policy, ghostwritten in part by the American Motorcycle Association (AMA). When the AMA published proposed ORV trail standards at the tail end of this process, professional foresters blasted them.

In July 1972, the Forest Service held many listening sessions in order to glean public sentiment on the issue. Many people spoke at these sessions, both for and against ORV use in the HNF. Despite the fact that the data gathering was not yet complete, HNF supervisor Girton stated that certainly some portion of the forest would be allotted to ORV users, enraging many who felt that he had made up his mind prematurely and without analyzing the biophysical evidence or listening to the majority of the public. When written comments were then solicited, they ran twenty to one against reopening a portion of the HNF to ORV use. Despite the widespread negative sentiment concerning ORVs in the HNF from both the lay public and professional foresters, Girton made the decision to proceed with a policy of ORV use in the HNF and announced that it might occur as early as September. Ferguson later described his reaction:

> In my mind this decision was just plain wrong for several reasons: data collection and analyses were incomplete; the public, generally, did not want the trails; professional foresters had counseled against the trails; and the fragile Indiana terrain could not support the trails. We were kowtowing to one special interest group: the AMA, who, by the way, had bought Girton's two children trail bikes.

In December 1972, the state of Indiana published a report concluding that ORV use was not compatible with the natural resource purposes of the state properties and therefore continued its closure of state properties to ORVs. On the federal side, the Forest Service decided in 1973 to write an environmental impact statement (EIS) and propose rules regulating ORV usage in limited terrains. Frustrated with the closed doors he was facing with Girton, Ferguson took guerrilla action and submitted comments expressing his professional view against ORV trails through the national environmental group Citizens for a Better Environment. Ferguson explained:

> By the time the final EIS was written and distributed in 1974, the original ORV trail standards had been removed, language had been watered down, and trail standards developed by the AMA—which arrived after the cutoff date for responses—were published as an appendix to the EIS. The public response to this unpopular decision was as expected—people were outraged, and my phone rang off the hook with calls from angry citizens.

In response to the EIS, the Indiana division of the Izaak Walton League of America (IWL), of which Ferguson was a member, filed an administrative appeal with the regional forester requesting that the policy be set aside. Ferguson helped draft the appeal. Before responding to the IWL appeal, in August 1974, the Forest

Service launched a crash project to construct and open ORV trails in the HNF by October 14, 1974. The IWL reacted by requesting a stay of construction from the regional forester pending a decision on the administrative appeal. The regional forester denied the stay on October 2, 1974.

Trail construction commenced without advance approval as required by Forest Service regulations, and without the required preapproved project plans. The Forest Service regulations in effect at the time required advance approval from the regional forester, on an individual-project basis, for all grades with slopes in excess of 15 percent. Several such grades were completed on this project prior to any submission of the construction plans for the regional forester's approval. The survey and design were conducted simultaneously with construction, contrary to the federal requirement that plans be completed and approved prior to construction. Ferguson explained:

> I witnessed these trails being built illegally with $34,000 of public money that was budgeted for routine maintenance of roads and trails. The Forest Service's own guidance on financial planning for that fiscal year clearly said, in regard to forest roads and trails appropriation: "Forest supervisors have no authority to make fund adjustments between the maintenance and construction activities of the Forest Roads and Trails appropriation."[3] The Hoosier National Forest budgets had been severely reduced already for fiscal years 1974 and 1975. This reduction was particularly severe for the Forest Roads and Trails appropriation. The budget cuts forced a reduction in force in engineering personnel and were barely sufficient for routine maintenance of the then-existing roads and trails systems. The contractor who did the work was told to bill the Forest Service for "routine maintenance." To divert these funds for the pet project of one man was clearly against the public will and a violation of law. I was outraged.

FERGUSON DECIDES
TO SUE THE FOREST SERVICE

On October 9, 1974, Forest Supervisor Girton and District Ranger Frank Haubry conducted a field trip for the HNF staff to review the newly constructed ORV trails. Ferguson was one of those on the field trip. They met at an assembly point and proceeded to drive the two-track trail system in four-wheel-drive vehicles. They examined small segments of the one-track system by short hikes on foot. Ferguson's reaction:

> I was appalled. I personally observed violations of the president's executive order as well as flagrant violations of the Forest Service's trail standards. For example, roads and trails were located and constructed to damage soil and watershed on lands acquired for the protection of streams. Vegetation had been removed and destroyed during the construction, and more damage was imminent from the proposed use on lands acquired for the production of timber. Trails were located on land acquired especially for wildlife habitat and public

hunting and specially developed by the Indiana Department of Natural Resources using hunter firearms tax money under the Pittman-Robertson Wildlife Restoration Act.[4]

These trails were located in one of the most significant wildlife habitat areas in the state of Indiana and in one of the very few wild turkey and ruffed grouse ranges in the state. The trails were located where significant conflicts would result with other existing recreational uses—primarily hunting, hiking, and horseback riding. It was evident that very little consideration had been given to the effects of noise and exhaust pollution on the forest, water, and wildlife. I observed violations of regulations for reverse curves, trail grades, and minimum safe stopping sight distance. I observed stumps that were not flush cut in the middle of ORV trails. I observed fallen logs, up to six inches in diameter, that were left in place across trails. I observed many areas requiring trail surfacing that were not surfaced.

My most serious concern, however, was this: given the fact that there was no age limit for ORVs on these trails, they posed one of the most serious threats to public safety—especially to the very young—that I had ever witnessed on public land paid for with public funds. Liability [tort] claims were certain to be filed against the Forest Service, and lives could be lost—with the blessing of the Forest Service. I could not live with the thought of a child losing his or her life because of our negligence or inaction.

At the conclusion of the field trip the group assembled in a parking lot for commentary. I expressed that I was "professionally sick" with what I had just seen: it was truly the most sickening thing I had seen in my career. I recited some of the violations I had seen and asked how any of us could defend what we had done when queried by the public. Mr. Girton dismissed my remarks by stating that they were one man's opinion. I immediately called my contacts at the IWL and told them that if they truly were going to sue the Forest Service over the ORV trails, as we had discussed at an earlier date, to count me in as a supporter.

Box 4.1 Claude Ferguson's Clashing Obligations

---

1. Forest Service Regulation 6173.53h (1974): " Involvement in Public Controversies. Employees are expected to avoid becoming involved in public controversies on matters of public policy. Disagreements as to either fact or policy should not, under any circumstances, be publicly aired through statements to the press or any other medium. . . . "

2. Code of Ethics for Government Service (1974): " Any person in Government service should: Put loyalty to the highest moral principles and to country above loyalty to persons, party or Government department. . . . "

(Continued)

Box 4.1 (Continued)

3. Part 735 Employees' Responsibility and Conduct, Title 7 Agriculture, Subtitle A—Office of the Secretary of Agriculture, Subpart E (1974)—Conduct Prohibited conduct—general:

   (b) (10) Taking any action which might prejudice the Government's interest in a criminal or civil case;

   (b) (11) Giving aid or assistance, other than in the discharge of official duties, to any claimant in prosecuting any claim against the United States;

   (b) (12) (ii) Directly or indirectly condemn or criticize the policies of any Government department or agency.

Excerpt from the affidavit of A. Claude Ferguson; *Indiana Division, Izaak Walton League of America Endowment, Inc. vs. Donald Girton, Supervisor, Wayne-Hoosier National Forest, Indiana, and Jay Cravens, Easter Region Forester, United States Forest Service*:

At this point I respectfully remind the Court that I am an employee of the Forest Service, United States Department of Agriculture. I am subject to the Employee Responsibilities and Conduct [rules] as set forth in Office of Personnel Regulations Part 735. . . . I am torn between my responsibilities to citizens (Subpart A) for whom I serve as a professional manager of their resources and the prohibition against prejudicing the Government's interest in a criminal or civil case (Subpart B (b) (10))."

On October 13, 1974, Ferguson conducted a field trip to the ORV trails that several members of the public, including environmentalists and reporters, attended. That same day, he also participated in a meeting of the Indiana Conservation Council. According to the minutes of that meeting:

Claude Ferguson reported on the latest developments in the Nebo Ridge area. (The Nebo Ridge area is a pristine wilderness area in Indiana that several of us were trying to keep in its natural state.) He mentioned that he would be working with a conservation group in formulating plans to initiate a suit to close the Hoosier National Forest to ORV use. He also mentioned that The Nature Conservancy will begin a fund drive to obtain money to purchase key tracts of land in the Nebo Ridge area so that it can be preserved as a wilderness. (*Indiana Conservation Council Newsletter,* October 1974)

On October 16, 1974, an article authored by a reporter named Don Jordan appeared in the local paper, the *Bedford Daily Times-Mail.* Ferguson was quoted as follows when asked his opinion about the ORV trails system: "You can quote me as being professionally sick. . . . This is the most sickening thing I've seen in 30 years of service" (Jordan 1974). The following day, Don Girton confronted him and asked if the quote was accurate. When Ferguson said it was, Girton handed him a copy of the part of the Forest Service manual that deals with involvement in public controversies. Ferguson later offered to send the newspaper the following clarification:

> The statements ascribed to me were my own professional opinion and were not intended to, nor did they, represent official condemnation or criticism of any policy of my employer. I regret that they may have been so misconstrued and hereby retract any such connotation.

Girton would not allow Ferguson to take such action, later explaining to a special agent of the Department of Agriculture that he felt the disclaimer "would tend to compound the public misunderstanding about the Forest Service's position in the matter" (affidavit of Donald Girton to Special Agent Richard E. Turner, in U.S. Department of Agriculture 1975).[5]

The IWL then filed suit in federal court on October 19, 1974, seeking a temporary restraining order and an injunction halting the trails. An affidavit Ferguson authored documenting the damage to the ORV trails (complete with evidence collected with the assistance of volunteers from Indiana University) was attached to the request for the restraining order (see Box 4-2). The restraining order and injunction were granted on October 24, 1974.

Box 4.2 Excerpts from the Affidavit of A. Claude Ferguson

Indiana Division, Izaak Walton League of America Endowment, Inc. vs. Donald Girton, Supervisor, Wayne-Hoosier National Forest, Indiana, and Jay Cravens, Easter Region Forester, United States Forest Service

A. CLAUDE FERGUSON, Being duly sworn, deposes and says:
1. He is a member of the Indiana Division, Izaak Walton League of America. . . .
4. This Preliminary Injunction should be granted because:

> As a professional in the natural resource management field, I am ashamed of the off-road vehicle policy and the trail layout and design being implemented on the Hoosier National Forest in Indiana. It is the

(Continued)

Box 4.2 (Continued)

most sickening thing I have witnessed in my 30-year career. I share this opinion with colleagues of the several other natural resource professions.

As a land use planner of many years in six states, I find the allocation for this use of the limited and fragile public lands in the sensitive Norman and Crawford Uplands of Indiana most contrary to all wise land use planning principles. . . . Construction of the trail system is currently damaging the timber, wildlife habitat and watershed values of the Forest and conflicting with wildlife and previously established extensive recreation uses of the forest. . . .

As a hunter who has willingly supported and paid my eleven (11) percent excise tax on sporting arms and ammunition into the Pittman-Robertson Wildlife Restoration Fund, I am angered to see the wildlife waterholes and openings . . . now converted to more road and motorcycle trail use. . . . Considering the very limited ruffed grouse and wild turkey ranges in Indiana and the many areas presently and potentially available for motorized vehicles, it seems a grave error to insert vehicle use into the erosive hills of this limited grouse and turkey range. Myself and every other citizen of Indiana is damaged by this action.

From my association with the laymen who initiated the Enabling Act to establish the National Forests of Missouri and who established the Missouri Conservation Commission during the second wave of conservation in the early 1930s, I know these fellows and their counterparts in Indiana would be saddened with this use of the lands they loved. This action is contrary to all expressions of purpose as stated to me by these giants of stature and stamina. As passing custodian of their trust and faith, I claim grave damage for them, myself and for our generations to come.

As one long concerned with public safety and especially with child safety, I am horrified with the roads and trails as now constructed and with the lack of controls. . . .

. . . [I]t is apparent that expenditures for this activity are most unwise and constitute a gross misuse of public funds. . . .

In summary, I claim . . . damage from . . . loss of national forest timber production, . . . watershed quality, . . . wildlife habitat and production, . . . other recreation uses, . . . loss of funds previously invested in timber and wildlife projects in affected areas, loss from fires resulting from increased hazard and risk, loss from any torts claims awarded as a result of this action, loss of motor fuels expended . . . , loss of tax dollars. . . .

After learning that Ferguson had filed the affidavit in the federal court suit, Girton wrote to the regional forester:

We are now faced with the immediate task of working with the U.S. Attorney to prepare for a hearing within the next 20 days. It will be extremely difficult for my staff to work with the U.S. Attorney to prepare a case that will involve confidential communications when a key member of my staff has signed an affidavit in support of the plaintiff's position. (U.S. Department of Agriculture 1975)

Five days later, Girton informed Ferguson that the regional forester was sending Ferguson to Milwaukee to work in the Fire and Aviation Management Group, and that his initial detail would be for three weeks, from November 4 through November 22, 1974. Girton later put in writing that he considered this detail "a possible temporary solution to the problem" and "timely." Ferguson's response: "I considered the detail to be harassment and punishment for exercising my constitutional right to free speech, as well as a shallow cover for my fraudulent removal from office. I refused to go" (U.S. Department of Agriculture 1975).

After the regional forester denied the IWL appeal in January 1975, the American Motorcycle Association joined the lawsuit on behalf of the Forest Service. Guerrilla warfare was in full force. The Sassafras (Indiana) chapter of the Audubon Society, the National Audubon Society, the Indiana Conservation Council (the National Wildlife Federation affiliate in Indiana), and the National Wildlife Federation joined the lawsuit supporting the Izaak Walton League.

WILL FERGUSON BE TRANSFERRED?

On March 3, 1975, Ferguson was given notice that he was to be transferred permanently to Milwaukee, where he had been "selected" for a GS-12 position to begin on April 13. On April 3, 1975, he wrote to Don Girton and Carl Webb, director of personnel management for the Forest Service in Milwaukee, stating his refusal to be transferred, especially given the fact that the Forest Service refused to transfer his wife, who was also a Forest Service employee. The IWL appealed the ORV case to the Board of Forest Appeals on April 4, 1975, and waited eight months for a denial of appeal from the board.

On April 9, 1975, Girton received a memo from Webb that read, in part:

Claude has made public statements regarding Forest Service policies that have brought criticism against the Forest Service. The public has difficulty differentiating from Forest Service policy and Mr. Ferguson's personal views. Since one of his key duties as a Forest Staff Officer involves the Information and Education program, we feel there is a situation that may result in continued conflict of interest. There have been recent complaints about his statement and actions regarding the proposed Eastern Wilderness Legislation. We conclude that this reassignment is warranted to preclude continuation of this problem. (from Claude Ferguson's personal files)

On May 19, 1975, Ferguson received a memorandum from Webb indicating that his transfer to Milwaukee was being delayed pending an investigation, but that he would be detailed on May 27, 1975. On May 20, Ferguson received a second memorandum stating that the effective date of the detail to Milwaukee had been moved to June 2.

That same month, May 1975, Ferguson received an award from the Indiana Sassafras Audubon Society commending his "extraordinary efforts in the preservation of our natural resources." The commendation read in part:

> Claude Ferguson is a seasoned forester who is a staff officer in the management of the Hoosier National Forest. For thirty-two years he has served well the interests of us all in the United States Forest Service. We salute him today not for any single accomplishment, although many could be cited. Rather, we want to commend him for a career-long demonstration of sensitivity and concern for the preservation of our natural environment.
>
> Most of us find that our own interests often conflict with those of other people in our society. Mr. Ferguson labors within a milieu where those conflicting forces have to be balanced. He performs there with a grace and gentle spirit that must be admired. He maintains both a personal and vocational love for the kind of world that Audubon members strive to achieve and pass on to subsequent generations. For this we thank him.

Soon after this, an opinion survey released by the Forest Service for the Midlands Area reported that 63 percent of the Forest Service personnel who replied to a question on whether ORVs should be allowed in the forests believed that they should be prohibited. Only 6 percent felt they should have been allowed (letter from Thomas E. Dustin, executive secretary, Indiana division of the IWL, to J. Carl Ferguson, father of Claude Ferguson, July 24, 1975; from Claude Ferguson's personal files). Ferguson broadened his guerrilla attack, and government officials reacted. Ferguson described the events that followed:

> I then asked the Office of Inspection within the Forest Service to investigate my case. They ended up investigating only my complaints of harassment, fraud, and deceit in connection with my detail to the regional office in Milwaukee (and found my detail to be "reasonable"). Two of my colleagues went on record accusing me of being mentally ill. One used confidential medical records of an illness I had had years ago as "proof" that I was mentally unstable [from U.S. Department of Agriculture 1975]. . . . The investigator was told not to look into my charges of wrongdoing connected to the ORV issue because it was a subject being considered in the civil action in court.

In June 1975, Ferguson submitted a report to the Office of Inspection within the Forest Service that documented wrongdoing in the development of the ORV trails. He received no response to that report. After being suspended from the Forest Service for two weeks without pay, Ferguson was then notified that he would be removed from office, effective February 15, 1976, for participating in a lawsuit in which the government had an interest, and for conflict of interest. This was eighteen months before he would have been eligible for retirement. Ferguson explained:

> I asked for early retirement instead, but my request was denied, putting me in jeopardy of losing up to $300,000 in pension benefits due me for thirty-four years of service. I immediately held a press conference protesting my treatment and filed a request with the secretary of agriculture for a full investigation. "As of Monday I will join the ranks of the unemployed," the local paper quoted me as saying. "I regret this loss of protection for my family, but honor has no price tag in our circles" [Snapp 1976].

The City Council of Bedford, Indiana, headquarters of the HNF, passed a unanimous resolution requesting that a fair and impartial investigation of Ferguson's treatment be made (Joseph 1976a). That resolution was sent to John R. McGuire, chief of the Forest Service; Edward H. Levi, attorney general of the United States; and U.S. Congressman Phil Hayes. An editorial in a local newspaper commented, "It is a sad state of affairs when an employee of government is prohibited from speaking out on something that is obviously wrong, and then fired if he does so" (*Bedford Daily Times-Mail,* February 12, 1976). Another newspaper wrote: "Claude Ferguson, whose career in the U.S. Forest Service apparently ends tomorrow, belongs to the rare breed of government employe [*sic*] who recognizes that his ultimate responsibility is to his conscience and to the public. . . . What confronted Mr. Ferguson was a conflict between what he considered the greater public good and a Forest Service policy" ("Claude Ferguson: A Whistle-Blower Gets the Axe," *Louisville Courier-Journal and Times,* February 15, 1976).

Additional protests were voiced by the Indiana Sassafras Audubon Society, the Indiana division of the Izaak Walton League, the Indiana Conservation Council, the Nebo Ridge Study Committee, the Sierra Club, and the student committee of the Indiana Sassafras Audubon Society. "It is a question of whether public servants serve the public or their immediate supervisors," commented Phil Schrodt of the student committee of the Indiana Sassafras Audubon Society (Young 1976). (Regarding Ferguson's clashing obligations, see Box 4.1. See Boxes 4.3 and 4.4 for letters against and in support of Ferguson, respectively.) Ferguson explained further: "My family rallied around me. My father contacted Congressman Richard Ichord of Missouri, while my daughter wrote the president of the United States. I continued to write policy makers around the country, including Congressman John Dingell, Agriculture Secretary Robert Bergland, and Attorney General Bell."

Box 4.3 Excerpts of Letters of Complaint about Claude Ferguson

---

October 24, 1974

To Donald Girton, Hoosier National Forest Supervisor

. . . Mr. Claude Ferguson of the U.S. Forest Service has openly aligned himself with the Izaak Walton League in opposition to the use of National Forest for motorcycle trails. We object to this involvement lest it be construed that the U.S. Forest Service has taken a stand supporting this opposition.

> Louis C. Broering, Hope, Indiana; E. Glen Davidson, Seymour, Indiana;
> Ronald W. Scheffel, Columbus, Indiana

October 30, 1974

To Jay H. Cravens, Regional Forester

. . . [W]e are dismayed to learn of the most recent actions of one of the Hoosier National Forest's staff, Claude Ferguson. Mr. Ferguson has consistently acted not as an employee of a governmental agency ultimately responsible to the tax paying citizens, but has consistently pursued his own personal convictions and opinions. . . . [His actions] portray an active individual interest in a publicity campaign which he engineered to ban trail bikes from the Hoosier. . . . On behalf of our membership in Indiana and our national membership we respectfully demand that Mr. Ferguson be permanently removed from the employ of the United States Forest Service.

> Gene Wirwahn, Legislative Director, American Motorcycle Association

May 20, 1975

To Donald Girton, Forest Supervisor

I read in the May 10, 1975, *Bloomington Herald-Telephone* about the "good guy" award given Claude Ferguson by the Sassafras Chapter of the Audubon Society. My heart immediately went out to you "not so good guys" who have conscientiously attempted to work with their peers and carry out the directions of their superiors in order that the American public could receive maximum benefits from the nation forest lands. . . . [About the ORV controversy], I happen to be on Claude's side, but I don't understand why the Forest Service has permitted him to publicly and actively pursue a policy contradictory to their formal policy.

There has to be a conflict of interest. Surely Claude participated in the decision making process when the Forest Service policy was being formulated, and I'm sure his opinions received the same consideration as those of his peers. Once the Forest Service reached a decision, I don't understand Claude being permitted to publicly espouse his personal conflicting opinions. I admire and respect individuals who have the courage to stick to their convictions, but for their organizations to permit them to do so in contradiction to the organization's publicized position is most unusual. Do you know of any other government agency that permits this? Certainly not the Armed Forces or the Defense Department! Are all Forest Service employees permitted this latitude? In my experience there is no private business that would tolerate it for one minute.

Harry Hollis, Bedford, Indiana

Source: U.S. Department of Agriculture 1975.

Box 4.4 Excerpts of Letters in Support of Claude Ferguson

February 16, 1976

It seems to me that the leadership of the Forest Service is more concerned with beating down responsible dissent within the service than in managing the forest resources in a responsible way. I have walked the trails that the Forest Service intends to open to the use of the public for trail bike riding. I know that those trails are very dangerous. Many lawsuits can be expected from riders being injured by the negligent manner in which the trails were constructed. It is obvious that this was a result of an unrealistic deadline and incompetent workers. The leadership of the Forest Service must take responsibility for this atrocious situation. They have brought dishonor to an institution that has a noble history. For this same leadership to try to place the blame for this sad state of affairs on a man with a long and honorable career who felt required to speak out is both unethical and unconscionable.

Bill Hayden, Bedford, Indiana (_Bedford Daily Times-Mail,_ February 16, 1976)

(Continued)

Box 4.4 (Continued)

February 19, 1976

I can not understand why the U.S.F.S. could, under any circumstances, give way to ORV's or any other special interests. Such activities within the forest will surely disrupt over-all tranquility let alone the negative effect it will have on the grouse and turkey populations. After all, if a group wanted to build a baseball park in the forest, would that also be OK?

Along the same line, I can not really understand why A. Claude Ferguson is having so much trouble with your agency. . . . All the people of Bedford, Indiana, are concerned about this matter and we all will be watching the outcome of . . . [Ferguson's] case with the U.S.F.S. with great interest.

> P. Decker Major, Wildlife Biologist, Grouse-Turkey Research,
> Indiana Department of Natural Resources

February 24, 1976

. . . [T]he crux of the issue is whether a responsible civil servant ought to be fired for calling attention to specific wrongdoings in the implementation of government programs."

> Jenifer Robison, Bloomington, Indiana
> (*Indiana Daily Student,* February 24, 1976)

When questioned by the press, Forest Supervisor Girton commented: "I guess it goes back to this old adage—if you must condemn and you must criticize externally, I think it gets to the point where the individual had better just resign his position and pursue his course of action—if he feels that strongly about it" (Holwager 1976). To another reporter, Girton commented, "Employes [*sic*] have to refrain from directly or indirectly criticizing the rules of the agency" (Jordan 1976). Later, Girton said that Ferguson had always been against the idea of ORV use in the forest and that he "disguised" his beliefs so he could attack the policy (Lindley 1976).

It is important to note that around this time Girton publicly admitted to certain trail deviations (Joseph 1976b). Congressman Phil Hayes asked the Public Integrity Section of the U.S. Department of Justice to review Ferguson's case. He also sent letters of support to John R. McGuire, chief of the Forest Service; Edward Levi, attorney general; and L. Lucius Free, assistant director of the Office of

Investigation of the U.S. Department of Agriculture. When asked to comment on Hayes's actions, Ferguson stated, "When the bright morning sunshine reaches the dark corners in this case, I am confident that the dust and cobwebs will become highly visible to those whose duty is to keep our house of government clean and in good order" ("Hayes Is Requesting Review of Ferguson Case," *Indianapolis Star,* February 17, 1976).

In June 1976, Ferguson received a "conservation service citation" from the National Wildlife Federation "for outstanding and distinguished service in the field of natural resource management." It was accompanied by a citation that described him as "a professional in every respect." The citation went on: "A trained, experienced, dedicated forester and wildlife manager, Ferguson found himself in a position where he was caught between his own moral convictions and professional responsibilities on one side and a decision from his own agency on the other. He made the hard choice—to follow his own moral and professional dictates." It continued:

> Claude was enough of a professional to go through all of the prescribed channels to convince his agency that its course of action was wrong. When this failed to produce results, he turned to the people who, in reality, are the owners of the natural resources involved. This entailed certain risks to Claude and his professional career; brought harassment and personal indignities, official censure and personal hardships, ostracism and substantial loss of income and earned retirement rights. Claude Ferguson laid his career and his professional well-being on the line for what he thought was right, and we have no doubts that history will prove that he was right.

The citation also quoted Abraham Lincoln, "To sin by silence when one should protest makes cowards out of men," and the second credo of Sigma Delta Chi, the national professional journalism fraternity, "He serves best who serves the truth." At that same meeting, Ferguson was given a plaque from the Indiana Conservation Council that said, "For outstanding service, loyalty, and devotion to conservation in Indiana—1976 Award" (*Bloomington Herald-Telephone,* August 3, 1976).

On July 17, 1976, at the national convention of the Izaak Walton League of America in Baltimore, Ferguson received a conservation award for "steadfast devotion to . . . high personal standards as a professional forester and a defender of soil, woods, water and wildlife, without regard for his own personal comfort and economic security" (*Bloomington Herald-Telephone,* August 3, 1976). In August 1976, Ferguson received an Environmental Quality Award from the U.S. Environmental Protection Agency for being a "citizen activist." He had been nominated for the award by the Bloomington, Indiana, chapter of the Sierra Club. In their letter of nomination, the Sierra Club members wrote that by protesting illegal ORV trails Ferguson had put his "loyalty to citizen ideals and professional principles above loyalty to the department which he had served faithfully for 33 years" ("Forester Ferguson on EPA 'Honor Roll,'" *Bloomington Herald-Telephone,* August 3, 1976).

As public opinion grew in his favor,[6] Ferguson requested that the U.S. Civil Service Commission hearing concerning his firing be held in his hometown of Bedford, Indiana. It was convened in December 1976 by a hearing officer from the U.S. Civil Service Commission. Ferguson's attorney, David Mosier, city judge of Columbus, Indiana, and president of the Indiana chapter of the Nature Conservancy, had subpoenaed the Forest Service chief of personnel from Washington, D.C., the regional forester, the assistant regional forester, and the Forest Service chief of personnel from Milwaukee, among others. Ferguson described it as follows:

> After consultations with my attorney, family, friends, and some colleagues, I had concluded that the best thing for all would be my reinstatement to the full retirement I had requested when I was first notified of my transfer to Milwaukee. Forest Service regulations allowed such action. I was tired and worn out by the battle, but wanted it to end justly and honorably. More importantly, I did not want to harm my coworkers or bring more controversy to the Forest Service I loved by being reinstated and then working side by side with Girton and others who had opposed me.
>
> I am certain that heads would have rolled if the hearing into my removal went full course. That I did not want. There were a handful that deserved such a "comeuppance," as grandmother would say, but the majority of those who would have been injured were good people who were caught between the proverbial rock and hard place—victims of the bureaucratic squeeze.
>
> Following the opening of the hearing, my attorney suggested a recess so that he might have a private conversation with the Forest Service chief of personnel, whom he had just met. The recess was granted by the greatly relieved hearing officer. David Mosier suggested to the chief of personnel that the two of them take a stroll around the block. Away they went, leaving a room full of very nervous and apprehensive bureaucrats. After perhaps fifteen minutes, the strollers returned. They approached the hearing officer, and the three of them talked quietly for a few minutes. The hearing officer then reopened the hearing to announce that the proceedings were completed.
>
> David came over to me and announced in a loud voice, "Claude, enjoy your well-earned retirement and let's get out of this place. I need some fresh air!" Later David told me he had recited just a little of the evidence we were going to present to the chief of personnel and told him of some of the witnesses we had ready to testify. The top Forest Service officials quietly folded their tent and slipped quietly into the night when they came face-to-face with the reality of the facts. My retirement benefits and other fringe benefits were restored retroactive to the date of my firing.

THE ORV COURT CASE CONTINUES

The ORV court challenge, however, continued to drag on. In May 1977, Judge William Steckler announced that a pretrial conference in the ORV case would be held in one month. The conference was held, and a trial date was set for the first week of December. By mid-October, information leaked to the press indicated that the Forest Service was ready to settle the lawsuit by withdrawing the entire policy allowing ORVs in the Hoosier National Forest (Ellis 1977; Snapp 1977a). At the end of October 1977, the Forest Service announced that it would indeed reconsider its ORV policy, a move that would settle the ORV case before it went to trial (Snapp 1977b; "Forest Service Restudies Off-Road Vehicle Policy," *Indianapolis Star,* October 29, 1977), and later it completely terminated its policy of allowing ORVs in the Hoosier National Forest.

Elated, Ferguson held a press conference with the four plaintiffs in the ORV case. Ferguson said it had been a "long, costly and heartbreaking three years that need not have been." He also asked for an investigation of some yet-to-be-answered questions:

> What about the apparent collusion between certain Forest Service officials and officials of the American Motorcycle Association in generating evidence to be used against me? What about the contempt of Forest Service officials in failing to respond to questions about this matter? What about the origin, timing, and erroneous content of the letters of complaint against me and my wife that were secured and used by the Forest Service officials from officers and members of the Citizens Concerned about the Nebo Ridge area? What about the character assassination attempt against me by one high Forest Service official by use of part of my medical record in violation of rules, regulations, and laws? (Snapp 1977c)

Almost simultaneously, Congressmen Morris K. Udall and Paul Simon, along with Senator Patrick J. Leahy, introduced bills in the U.S. Congress that would create review boards on improper governmental actions that would decide whether complaints or reports of government employees were made in good faith, and, if so, the employees making those complaints would be protected for two years from being harassed, fired, demoted, or given hardship transfers for speaking out. "I've been vindicated," said Ferguson.

Box 4.5 Kipling's "If" (given to Claude Ferguson by his father as "a code for his self-guidance")

If

> If you can keep your head when all about you
> Are losing theirs and blaming it on you;
> If you can trust yourself when all men doubt you,
> But make allowance for their doubting too;
> If you can wait and not be tired by waiting,
> Or, being lied about, don't deal in lies,
> Or, being hated, don't give way to hating,
> And yet don't look too good, nor talk too wise;

(Continued)

Box 4.5 (Continued)

If you can dream—and not make dreams your master;
If you can think—and not make thoughts your aim;
If you can meet with triumph and disaster
And treat those two imposters just the same;
If you can bear to hear the truth you've spoken
Twisted by knaves to make a trap of fools,
Or watch the things you gave your life to broken
And stoop and build 'em up with worn-out tools;

If you can make one heap of all your winnings
And risk it on one turn of pitch-and-toss,
And lose, and start again at your beginnings
And never breathe a word about your loss;
If you can force your heart and nerve and sinew
To serve your turn long after they are gone,
And so hold on when there is nothing in you
Except the Will which says to them: "Hold on"

If you can talk with crowds and keep your virtue,
Or walk with kings—nor lose the common touch;
If neither foes nor loving friends can hurt you;
If all men count with you, but none too much;
If you can fill the unforgiving minute
With sixty seconds' worth of distance run
Yours is the Earth and everything that's in it,
And—which is more—you'll be a Man my son!

—Rudyard Kipling

EPILOGUE

The use of off-road vehicles in the Hoosier National Forest is prohibited today. A 2011 study, however, expressed alarm at the growing number of illegal all-terrain vehicles (ATVs) in the HNF (Jasper 2011). The report concluded that ATVs were destroying vulnerable vegetation, causing erosion and soil compaction, creating ruts that were rerouting water flow patterns, producing sediment movement into streams, crushing aquatic life, depriving fish of oxygen, spreading nonnative invasive plants, and altering the entire ecosystem. A hotline has been established for the reporting of illegal ATV use in the Hoosier National Forest.

NOTES

1. All quotes are from 1999 interviews unless otherwise noted.

2. The address of Claude Ferguson's website is http://www.spoonplayer.com.

3. U.S. Department of Agriculture, "Forest Service Guidance on Planning," fiscal years 1974 and 1975.

4. The Pittman-Robertson Act—formally the Federal Aid in Wildlife Restoration Act—was approved by Congress on September 2, 1937, and went into effect on July 1, 1938. The purpose of this act was to provide funding for the selection, restoration, rehabilitation, and improvement of wildlife habitat; wildlife management research; and the distribution of information produced by the projects. The act was amended October 23, 1970, to include funding for hunter training programs and the development, operation, and maintenance of public target ranges. Funds are derived from an 11 percent federal excise tax on sporting arms, ammunition, and archery equipment and a 10 percent tax on handguns. Funds for hunter education and target ranges are derived from one-half of the tax on handguns and archery equipment. Each state's apportionment is determined by a formula that considers the total area of the state and the number of licensed hunters in the state.

5. The work cited is an official archival document of the U.S. Department of Agriculture. I obtained it from the personal papers of Claude Ferguson. It is also available in the archives of the U.S. District Court, Southern District of Indiana, Indianapolis, in the files of the case of *Indiana Division, Izaak Walton League of America Endowment, Inc. vs. Donald Girton,* or through the filing of a Freedom of Information Act request with the Department of Agriculture.

6. See, for example, "Opinion: Honors for a Trouble-Maker," *Louisville Courier-Journal and Times,* August 22, 1976. This editorial lauds "the conscientious attitude of A. Claude Ferguson" for putting loyalty to the highest moral principles and to country above loyalty to persons, party, or government department.

Third Interlude:
More Stories of Guerrilla
Government

FROM MOVIES to casual anecdotes to handbooks for advocates, the stories of guerrilla government continue.

GUERRILLA GOVERNMENT IN THE U.S. CENTRAL INTELLIGENCE AGENCY

The 2007 movie *Charlie Wilson's War* is about the flamboyant U.S. Congressman Charles Wilson of Texas and the private "war" he waged against the Soviets by secretly arranging for congressional appropriations to arm Afghan tribesmen with Stinger missiles and other combat gear. While the movie, based on the book by George Crile, a producer for the television newsmagazine *60 Minutes,* focuses primarily on Wilson, the most interesting character for the purposes of this book is Gust Avrakotos (played by Philip Seymour Hoffman), a government guerrilla who worked for the Central Intelligence Agency. After twice witnessing Wilson nearly single-handedly increase the CIA budget for its Afghan operations, Avrakotos violated the CIA's policy against lobbying Congress and, against the wishes of his superiors, asked Wilson for $50 million more. Working hand in hand with Avrakotos, Wilson was successful in obtaining not only the $50 million but also an additional $300 million in one year. But his clandestine guerrilla government work went far beyond funding the Afghan resistance. The *Washington Post* described Avrakotos in this way:

> Mr. Avrakotos, who ran the largest covert operation in the agency's history, was dubbed "Dr. Dirty" for his willingness to handle ethically ambiguous tasks and a "blue-collar James Bond" for his 27 years of undercover work. In the 1980s, [working with Charlie Wilson] he used Tennessee mules to bring hundreds of millions of dollars in automatic weapons, antitank guns and satellite maps from

Pakistan to the mujaheddin. Mr. Avrakotos eventually controlled more than 70 percent of the CIA's annual expenditures for covert operations, funneling it through intermediaries to the mujaheddin. As a result, the tribesmen drove the Soviets out of Afghanistan, and the long Cold War shuddered toward an end. Those weapons later were used in the fratricidal war in Afghanistan before the Taliban took control. Critics noted that those weapons probably were still in use, both in support of and against U.S. troops, when the United States went to war in Afghanistan in 2001. (Sullivan 2005)

Avrakotos and Wilson together helped persuade officials from Egypt, Pakistan, China, Israel, Saudi Arabia, and elsewhere to increase support for the cause. Avrakotos also clandestinely helped revamp the Afghans' tactics, logistics, and training. A harsh critic of Oliver North and the Iran-Contra arms-for-hostages affair, Avrakotos eventually was transferred to Africa and retired soon thereafter.

GUERRILLA GOVERNMENT IN THE U.S. DEPARTMENT OF HEALTH AND HUMAN SERVICES

Against the wishes of my division head, I lobbied my congressman on behalf of our program, the Administration on Aging, which is housed within the U.S. Department of Health and Human Services. I was mortified when I got caught and was reprimanded by the division head. My immediate superior, a midlevel manager, however, chastised me for being a wimp. "It's like my hunting dog and my rifle," he said. "I take my hunting dog out for long walks and surprise him by firing my rifle in the air. At first he jumped every time he heard the blast. Eventually he became immune to the sound and now does not get upset. You jumped the first time the rifle fired. Keep doing what you are doing . . . and eventually—like my dog—you will not notice the blast."

GUERRILLA GOVERNMENT IN THE QUEST TO PROTECT SCHOOL CHILDREN FROM PESTS AND PESTICIDES

In his book *A Worm in the Teacher's Apple* (2005), Marc Lame chronicles efforts to protect schoolchildren in the United States from the negative effects of dangerous pesticides. In one chapter he tells the story of "heroes and believers in government"—people who have stayed in government but worked around the system in order to do the right thing. The following is an excerpt:

> Rosemary O'Leary wrote an excellent article about the ability of . . . government workers to overcome, or in some cases subvert, the environmental policies or lack of policies which adversely affect the public. . . . In worst cases, some are

whistleblowers, but in most instances "believers" quietly, legally and ethically overcome the barriers erected by political appointees and anti-environmental lobbyists. I know government employees in local, state and USEPA Regional offices, as well as EPA headquarters in D.C. who, without agency policy or budgets, have been able to facilitate the progress we have made thus far [for the cause of protecting schoolchildren from pests and pesticides]. They used discretionary or generally directed funds under the authority of FIFRA [the Federal Insecticide, Fungicide, and Rodenticide Act]. For obvious reasons I leave most of their names out of print, but these are people like Carl Martin in Arizona, brave beyond belief in standing up to a state agency that was all but captive to the pest control industry. Charles Moses with the state of Nevada went to the local newspapers to embarrass the Las Vegas schools into trying IPM [integrated pest management]. Larry Swain with the state of Michigan developed the famous program at Cass Tech High School and has applied it to the neediest intercity areas in his state. Retired U.S. Environmental Protection Agency . . . [officials] Bill Curry, Ralph Wright and Jim Boland (who called me his favorite foil because my mouth was "protected") have worked behind the scenes for years at some risk to move IPM into schools. They have, at an average cost of less than three SUVs per state . . . been able to develop IPM in school informational materials (manuals, websites, brochures, etc.), training programs and demonstration models that affect millions of children. They have sometimes done this partnering with agency critics (offending administration supporters in the process) and working on their days off. They take risks and they fulfill their agency's mission to protect human health and the environment. (47)

GUERRILLA GOVERNMENT IN THE U.S. ARMY

Here is a story that happened last year where I work: Faced with a lack of sufficient funds to cover all legislative requirements for environmental compliance, in spring 2004 an Army Installation Management Activity general sent out an e-mail message urging all in his chain of command to cut costs wherever possible, to include taking "additional environmental risks." This was done without staff having any opportunity for open discussion of the issues and the expected changes before they took effect.

The e-mail message was leaked anonymously to several environmental groups, including Public Employees for Environmental Responsibility and the Natural Resources Defense Council. Incredibly, senior civilian army environmental officials had not been informed of the e-mail before it went public. There was a massive outcry both within and outside of the organization. The general ended up modifying his message the day the memo became public.

Why do something like this? Public agencies need to be accountable for their actions. The leaker may or may not be successful, but if the leak helps promote discourse on the issue, then the leak should be considered successful.

Why guerrilla government activity instead of going public? Not if you like your job! Go public once and you can never help undercover again. Use trusted contacts who guarantee anonymity, and who also trust the source.

GUERRILLA GOVERNMENT IN
A STATE DEPARTMENT OF TRANSPORTATION

I've worked for a state department of transportation for over two decades. In 2004, the department sued Amtrak for breach of contract. In my estimation the suit has no merit and can only serve to generate legal fees and hurt Amtrak. Explicitly in some cases and implicitly otherwise, we as DOT staff were told not to enter into contracts that would result in Amtrak being the beneficiary of capital projects. This was not a wise thing to do in my estimation, as Amtrak under David Gunn's leadership has done a great job repairing trains and filling seats despite political opposition.

For some time, for safety reasons I've been trying to install a more durable gate at a private rail crossing of Amtrak's line just south of [city]. Strictly speaking, this was probably betterment for Amtrak that I should have stayed away from. However, everyone here locally that I dealt with, including the Amtrak maintenance folk, with whom I have a strong positive working relationship, agreed that this was an important safety improvement that should be installed. So I arranged to have it done. Amtrak staff provided the necessary safety protection to the gate installer, but the state paid the bill. We made sure that payment went directly to the installer, not to Amtrak. It was the right thing to do to protect the public.

MORE GUERRILLA GOVERNMENT AT THE
U.S. ENVIRONMENTAL PROTECTION AGENCY

Here is an example of guerrilla government involving Val Adamkus, who at the time was administrator of the U.S. Environmental Protection Agency's Region 5, in Chicago. The case centered on a contested "dredge and fill" permit for a golf course proposed on private property adjacent to the Crystal River in Michigan (a wild and scenic river that runs through Sleeping Bear Dunes National Lakeshore). There was a lot of political intrigue in this episode, with interesting twists and turns. In short, Adamkus opposed the permit and refused a direct order to return permitting authority to the state of Michigan. Adamkus documented many of the details of the case in a letter he sent to EPA headquarters, knowing that the letter would be subject to Freedom of Information Act requests and would provide ammunition for an environmental group that also opposed the permit.

There is a happy ending to the Adamkus story. The permit was never issued, and the land was later obtained by the National Park Service in a land swap. The river remained wild and scenic, and Adamkus kept his job despite his fight with headquarters. He later retired from the EPA, gave up his U.S. citizenship, and returned to his native Lithuania, where he was elected to the presidency. By the way, he was a real guerrilla as a young man, fighting against the occupation of his country, first by the Germans and then by the Russians. Amazing guy.

WikiLeaks and Guerrilla Government: The World's Largest Security Breach

Hi. I'm an Army intelligence analyst. . . . I don't have anyone to talk to. . . . I can't believe what I'm telling you . . . an entire repository of classified foreign policy is available. . . . it affects everybody on earth.

And so began the e-mail of Private First Class Bradley Manning that unraveled his secret world as a government guerrilla who leaked hundreds of classified government documents to WikiLeaks, an organization that publishes online submissions of secret information, information leaks, and classified media from anonymous sources and whistle-blowers. Manning's actions have been called the largest security breach in the history of the world.

To truly understand the story of Private Manning becoming a government guerrilla, one needs to go back to rural Crescent, Oklahoma, where Manning was born in 1987. Various stories about his early years emphasize that he was a smart loner, a computer nerd, and a three-time winner of the high school science fair. "By middle school," the *Washington Post* reported, "Bradley was altering lines of code to transform a computer-game character's appearance, just for fun" (Nakashima 2011). He was a talented computer hacker who felt that he was socially ostracized for being different.

After graduating from high school, Manning floated around, holding jobs in a pizza parlor, a guitar center, a Starbucks, and an Abercrombie & Fitch store. After attending community college, he joined the army in 2007. Brian Manning, Bradley's father, told the PBS television program *Frontline* (February 28, 2011) that he encouraged his son to join the army,

> to get a sense of structure in his life. I said, "Bradley, you're not really going anywhere." . . . And I said, "If you get into a place like the army, you know,

you're going to have three square meals a day, you're going to have a place to sleep and a roof over your head. And as long as you follow the path, it's all you have to do."

With dreams of earning a Ph.D. in physics, Bradley also relished the idea of a free education through the GI Bill.

After basic training at Fort Leonard Wood in Missouri, Bradley went to intelligence school at Fort Huachuca, Arizona, where he received a top-secret security clearance. After he graduated he joined the Second Brigade, Tenth Mountain Division, at Fort Drum, New York. A *Washington Post* article concluded that he did not adapt well to military culture:

> In August 2009, a supervisor, Master Sgt. Paul D. Adkins, noted that he was showing signs of "instability" and required him to seek mental health counseling, according to an Army report. Manning received an initial screening but no regular therapy. . . . Adkins and a major discussed leaving Manning behind when the unit deployed to Iraq in the fall. But the Army was short on intelligence analysts in Iraq. Manning was clearly bright and his behavior had started to improve, so his superiors decided to send him. (Nakashima 2011)

Manning was sent to Forward Operating Base Hammer near Baghdad in Iraq. There he had access to databases used by the U.S. government to transmit classified information. He was adept at his job. By the time he returned home for a short leave three months later, Manning had been promoted a rank. This is when he apparently first confided to friends that he had encountered massive quantities of sensitive information while on the job—some of it in classified databases not directly related to the mission of his unit in Baghdad—and was considering passing the information to WikiLeaks (Poulsen and Zetter 2010). Later Manning would explain that in these databases he

> saw incredible things, awful things . . . things that belonged in the public domain, and not on some server stored in a dark room in Washington DC. . . . A database of half a million events during the Iraq war . . . explaining how the first world exploits the third, in detail. (Manning, instant message to Adrian Lamo, May 2010)

Manning downloaded the data onto a compact disc, avoiding detection by keeping a serious face while humming and lip-synching "to Lady Gaga songs to make it appear that he was using the classified computer's CD player to listen to music" (Shanker 2010).

Soon after Manning returned to Baghdad in February 2010, WikiLeaks began posting documents that appeared to have been leaked from inside the U.S. government, beginning with the "Reykjavik 13" cable. (See Box 5.1 for the full time line.) This cable was a private government report that documented, among other things, that when the Icelandic bank Landsbanki went bankrupt, foreign depositors were not going to be repaid because the Icelandic Depositors' and Investors' Guarantee Fund had already been drained of capital reserves and had no money left. Further, the government of Iceland refused to take on this liability on behalf of the guarantee fund—in part because of the financial crisis Iceland was experiencing.

Box 5.1 Bradley Manning and WikiLeaks Time Line

2009

October: Manning is sent to Iraq.
November: Manning finds Baghdad air strike video.
November: Manning contacts WikiLeaks.

2010

February 18: WikiLeaks releases so-called Reykjavik 13 cable, obtained from Manning.
March 15: WikiLeaks releases Defense Department report about WikiLeaks, obtained from Manning.
March 29: WikiLeaks releases State Department profiles, obtained from Manning.
April 05: WikiLeaks releases Baghdad air strike video, allegedly from Manning.
May 21–25: Manning and Adrian Lamo chat.
May 26: Manning is arrested in Iraq.
June 06: Wired publishes partial logs of Manning-Lamo chat.
July 05: Manning is charged. Allegations include exceeding his authorized access; adding unauthorized software to a network computer; and wrongfully copying to his personal computer and then transmitting a classified video, 50 classified State Department cables, 150 additional State Department cables, and a classified PowerPoint presentation.
July 25: WikiLeaks releases Afghan War logs, obtained from Manning.
July 29: Manning is transferred to the United States.
October 22: WikiLeaks releases Iraq War logs, obtained from Manning.
November 28: Newspapers publish U.S. diplomatic cables from WikiLeaks, allegedly from Manning.

2011

January: United Nations special rapporteur submits inquiry to United States about Manning.
March 1: Manning is charged with more offenses, including unauthorized use of the army's information system; causing the publishing of U.S. intelligence on the Internet, knowing that it would be accessible to the enemy; stealing 380,000 records; unauthorized possession of more than 700 memoranda; and unauthorized transmission of a classified memo.
December 16: Manning's Article 32 hearing begins.

2012

February 3: Manning is ordered to stand trial.

2013

January 9: Trial is scheduled to begin June 2013.

February 28: Manning enters guilty plea for ten of twenty-two charges

June 03: Manning's trial begins at Fort Meade, Maryland. Prosecutors seek to prove that some of the material leaked by Manning had been used by al-Qaeda in a propaganda video and also was found in Osama bin Laden's personal computer.

July 03: Prosecutors rest their case against Manning.

July 30: Manning found guilty of more than 20 violations, including several violations of the Espionage Act. He was found not guilty of aiding and abetting the enemy.

August 05: Sentencing hearings begin.

August 21: Manning sentenced to 35 years in prison.

But it was a video that Manning found in the judge advocate's online top-secret directory that was particularly disturbing to him. The video showed a U.S. military air strike on July 12, 2007, in which a helicopter fired on a group of men in Baghdad. One of the men in the group was a journalist, and two others were Reuters employees carrying cameras that the pilots mistakenly thought were anti-tank grenade launchers. The soldiers in the helicopter also fired on a van that stopped to help the injured members of the first group. In this second attack, two children in the van were wounded and their father was killed. (This video is available for viewing at http://www.collateralmurder.com.)

WikiLeaks named the video "Collateral Murder," and Julian Assange, founder and editor in chief of WikiLeaks, released it during a press conference at the National Press Club in Washington, D.C., on April 5, 2010. After the video went public, Manning sent an e-mail to an officer in Iraq in which he pointed out that it was the same version as the one stored on the military's classified Secure Internet Protocol Router Network (SIPRNet). Some have said that this seems to indicate that Manning wanted to be caught (Nicks 2012, 157–161).

In addition to the Baghdad air strike video, Manning reputedly transmitted to WikiLeaks a video of a 2009 air strike in Granai, Afghanistan; 500,000 army reports, known as the Iraq War logs and the Afghan War logs; and 251,000 U.S. diplomatic cables or reports. Of the diplomatic cables he passed to WikiLeaks, 6 percent are classified "secret," 40 percent are classified "confidential," and the rest are considered unclassified.

MANNING E-MAILS ANOTHER HACKER

On May 20, 2010, Manning contacted Adrian Lamo after reading a profile of him published in *Wired* magazine online. Lamo had been convicted in 2004 for hacking into the *New York Times* computer network. He had been profiled that day by Kevin Poulsen, a former hacker who had used Lamo as a source several times before. The two worked together: Lamo would hack into a system, tell the organization he had done it, using Poulsen as the contact person, and then offer to fix the organization's security for a sum of money.

Manning sent Lamo several encrypted e-mails. Unable to decrypt them, Lamo invited the anonymous sender to chat using instant messaging on America on Line. In a series of chats from May 21 through May 25, 2010, with Manning using the handle "bradass87," Manning told Lamo that he had leaked classified material. Below are excerpts of the instant messaging exchanges, as published by *Wired* magazine. It is interesting to note that in the beginning of the chats, the conversation was one-sided, with Manning repeatedly offering information apparently without being encouraged by Lamo.

May 21, 2010

bradass87: (1:41:12 P.M.)	hi
bradass87: (1:44:04 P.M.)	how are you?
bradass87: (1:47:01 P.M.)	im an army intelligence analyst, deployed to eastern Baghdad, pending discharge for "adjustment disorder" in lieu of "gender identity disorder"
bradass87: (1:56:24 P.M.)	im sure you're pretty busy . . .
bradass87: (1:58:31 P.M.)	if you had unprecedented access to classified networks 14 hours a day 7 days a week for 8+ months, what would you do?

According to official documents, Lamo replied several hours later. Before Manning started discussing the leaks, Lamo told him: "I'm a journalist and a minister. You can pick either, and treat this as a confession or an interview (never to be published) & enjoy a modicum of legal protection." They talked about restricted material in general, and then Manning made his first direct reference to the leaks: "This is what I do for friends," he wrote. He linked to a section of the May 21, 2010, version of Wikipedia's article on WikiLeaks, which described the WikiLeaks release in March that year of a Department of Defense report on WikiLeaks itself. He added, "The one below that is mine too." The section below in the same article referred to the "Collateral Murder" video.

Manning said he felt "isolated and fragile" and was reaching out to someone he hoped might understand:

May 22, 2010

bradass87: (11:49:02 A.M.)	im in the desert, with a bunch of hyper-masculine trigger happy ignorant rednecks as neighbors . . . and the only safe place i seem to have is this satellite internet connection
bradass87: (11:49:51 A.M.)	and i already got myself into minor trouble, revealing my uncertainty over my gender identity . . . which is causing me to lose this job . . . and putting me in an awkward limbo. . . .
bradass87: (11:52:23 A.M.)	at the very least, i managed to keep my security clearance (so far). . . .
bradass87: (11:58:33 A.M.)	and little does anyone know, but among this "visible" mess, theres the mess i created that no-one knows about yet.
bradass87: (12:15:11 P.M.)	hypothetical question: if you had free reign over classified networks for long periods of time . . . say, 8–9 months . . . and you saw incredible things, awful things . . . things that belonged in the public domain, and not on some server stored in a dark room in Washington DC . . . what would you do? . . .
bradass87: (12:21:24 P.M.)	say . . . a database of half a million events during the iraq war . . . from 2004 to 2009 . . . with reports, date time groups, lat-lon locations, casualty figures . . . ? or 260,000 state department cables from embassies and consulates all over the world, explaining how the first world exploits the third, in detail, from an internal perspective? . . .
bradass87: (12:26:09 P.M.)	lets just say *someone* i know intimately well, has been penetrating US classified networks, mining data like the ones described . . . and been transferring that data from the classified networks over the "air gap" [security wall] onto a commercial network computer . . . sorting the data, compressing it, encrypting it, and uploading it to a crazy white haired aussie who can't seem to stay in one country very long. . . .
bradass87: (12:31:43 P.M.)	crazy white haired dude = Julian Assange
bradass87: (12:33:05 P.M.)	in other words . . . ive made a huge mess :'(

Manning said he started to leak information to WikiLeaks around Thanksgiving in November 2009 after WikiLeaks had released the 9/11 pager messages. (These were communications sent during and after the terrorist attacks on New York City and Washington, D.C., on September 11, 2001, by individuals working for the Pentagon, the Federal Bureau of Investigation, the Federal Emergency Management Agency, and the New York Police Department, to name a few.) Manning told Lamo he recognized that the messages had come from a National Security Agency database, and that made him feel better about leaking his information. Lamo asked what kind of material he was dealing with, and Manning replied: "uhm . . . crazy, almost criminal political backdealings . . . the non-PR-versions of world events and crises." Although he said he dealt with Assange directly, he also said Assange had adopted a deliberate policy of knowing very little about him, telling Manning: "Lie to me."

May 22, 2010

bradass87: (1:11:54 P.M.)	and . . . its important that it gets out . . . i feel, for some bizarre reason
bradass87: (1:12:02 P.M.)	it might actually change something
bradass87: (1:13:10 P.M.)	i just . . . dont wish to be a part of it . . . at least not now . . . im not ready . . . i wouldn't mind going to prison for the rest of my life, or being executed so much, if it wasn't for the possibility of having pictures of me . . . plastered all over the world press . . . as [a] boy. . . .
bradass87: (1:14:11 P.M.)	i've totally lost my mind . . . i make no sense . . . the CPU is not made for this motherboard. . . .
bradass87: (1:39:03 P.M.)	i cant believe what im confessing to you :'(

At that point, Lamo again assured Manning that his words would be kept in confidence. Manning wrote: "but im not a source for you . . . im talking to you as someone who needs moral and emotional f*****g support," and Lamo replied: "i told you, none of this is for print."

Manning said the incident that affected him the most was when fifteen individuals had been arrested by the Iraqi Federal Police for printing anti-Iraqi literature. He was asked by the army to find out who the "bad guys" were, and he concluded that the "bad guys" were members of the corrupt Iraqi cabinet—not the detainees. Manning reported this to his commanding officer but was told he "didn't want to hear any of it." Manning said the officer told him to help the Iraqi police find more detainees. Manning said it made him realize, "i was actively involved in something that i was completely against." He continued: "I can't separate myself from others . . . i feel connected to everybody . . . like they were distant family," and cited astronomer Carl Sagan, theoretical physicist Richard Feynman, and Nobel laureate and Holocaust survivor Elie Wiesel as inspirational to him. Manning said he wanted the leaked material to catalyze "worldwide discussion, debates, and reforms. If not . . . then we're doomed as a species."

Manning explained that he had downloaded the material onto music CD-RWs, erasing the music and replacing it with compressed files. Part of the reason no one noticed, he said, was that staff were working fourteen hours a day, seven days a week. "People stopped caring after 3 weeks," he explained.

May 25, 2010

bradass87: (02:12:23 P.M.)	so . . . it was a massive data spillage . . . facilitated by numerous factors . . . both physically, technically, and culturally
bradass87: (02:13:02 P.M.)	perfect example of how not to do INFOSEC
bradass87: (02:14:21 P.M.)	listened and lip-synced to Lady Gaga's Telephone while exfiltratrating [*sic*] possibly the largest data spillage in american history. . . .
bradass87: (02:17:56 P.M.)	weak servers, weak logging, weak physical security, weak counter-intelligence, inattentive signal analysis . . . a perfect storm. . . .
bradass87: (02:22:47 P.M.)	i mean what if i were someone more malicious
bradass87: (02:23:25 P.M.)	i could've sold to russia or china, and made bank?
info@adrianlamo .com: (02:23:36 P.M.)	why didn't you?
bradass87: (02:23:58 P.M.)	because it's public data. . . .
bradass87: (02:24:46 P.M.)	it belongs in the public domain
bradass87: (02:25:15 P.M.)	Information should be free

Disturbed by what he had learned from Manning, Lamo went to Chet Uber of the nonprofit organization Project Vigilant, which researches cybercrime, as well as a friend who had worked in military intelligence. Both men advised Lamo to go to the FBI, and they both then contacted the U.S. Army Criminal Investigation Command. Lamo reached out to the FBI soon after his first chat with Manning on May 21, saying he believed Manning was endangering lives. Lamo sized up Manning in this way: "He was ideologically motivated from a position he saw as well-intentioned, and he represented his motive as social responsibility in the pursuit of a wider benefit regarding disclosure of certain information" (Hansen 2011).

On May 25, Lamo showed the chat logs to the FBI and the army. He also passed the story to his former coconspirator, Poulsen of *Wired.* On May 27, Manning was arrested in Iraq. Two weeks later, on June 7, 2010, the Pentagon issued the following statement:

> United States Division-Center is currently conducting a joint investigation of Specialist Bradley Manning, 22, of Potomac, Md., who is deployed with Second Brigade 10th Mountain Division, in Baghdad, Iraq. He was placed in pretrial confinement for reputedly releasing classified information and is currently confined in Kuwait. The Department of Defense takes the management of classified information very seriously because it affects our national security, the lives of our soldiers, and our operations abroad.

Later, the military prosecutor, Major Ashden Fein, would describe Manning's response to his arrest in Kuwait as losing control, "screaming, shaking, babbling. . . . He made two nooses" and checked "yes" on an intake form that asked whether he had ever considered suicide, writing "always planning never acting" (Savage 2012).

Lamo gave Poulsen the chat logs and Manning's name. Poulsen and a colleague broke the news of Manning's arrest in *Wired* on June 6. *Wired* published a portion of the chat logs on June 6 and 10, and the full logs in July 2011. WikiLeaks responded by condemning Lamo and Poulsen as "notorious felons, informers and manipulators." Lamo in turn insisted that Bradley Manning "was to a great extent manipulated by WikiLeaks" (Bumiller 2010).

REACTIONS VARY

The reactions to Manning's alleged actions and his arrest varied widely. The dissemination of the leaked material, particularly the diplomatic cables, attracted in-depth news coverage around the world, with several governments blocking websites that contained embarrassing details. For example, one of the leaked cables describes a meeting between General David Petraeus, then the commander of U.S. Central Command, and Yemen's president in which they were discussing what was apparently a U.S. bombing campaign against al-Qaeda in the Arabian Peninsula. According to the cable, Yemeni president Ali Abdullah Saleh began to "joke that he had just 'lied'" by telling his parliament that the Yemeni forces were responsible for attacks carried out by the United States. "We'll continue saying the bombs are ours, not yours," the cable quotes Saleh as saying. Alan Rusbridger (2011), editor of the British newspaper the *Guardian,* wrote:

> I can't think of a time when there was ever a story generated by a news organization where the White House, the Kremlin, Chávez, India, China, everyone in the world was talking about these things. . . . I've never known a story that created such mayhem that wasn't an event like a war or a terrorist attack.

One of Manning's biographers concluded that Manning was viewed as both a twenty-first-century Tiananmen Square–like hero and a crazed traitor (Nicks 2012). Others asked why an apparently unstable army private had access to classified material, and why no security measures were in place to prevent unauthorized downloads (editorial, *Washington Post*, November 30, 2010). Still others called Manning the most important whistle-blower since Daniel Ellsberg leaked the Pentagon Papers in 1971 (Greenwald 2011). In fact, Ellsberg came out in full support of Manning, saying: "I identify with him very much. He sees the wars in Iraq and Afghanistan, I'd say correctly, as I saw Vietnam—as hopeless ventures that are wrong and involve a great deal of atrocities" (Shane 2011).

PayPal, banks, and credit card companies refused to do business with WikiLeaks and would not process payments to the virtual organization. Yet while major corporations condemned WikiLeaks, "Free Bradley Manning" support groups were cropping up around the world. By August 2012, more than 12,000 people had donated a total of $650,000 to the Bradley Manning Support Network, including $15,100 from WikiLeaks.

Manning was nominated for the Nobel Peace Prize in 2011, 2012, and 2013. Nominators included the Oklahoma Center for Conscience and Peace Research and three members of the Icelandic parliament. Readers of the *Guardian* voted him 2012 person of the year.

In the meantime, for a nine-month period Manning was locked in a six-by-twelve-foot cell, stripped of his clothes and glasses because he was considered a suicide risk, and isolated from other inmates for twenty-three hours a day. His lawyer said that he became very weak because of the lack of exercise and that his emotional health had deteriorated, triggering depression and anxiety. A United Nations torture investigator attempted an unmonitored visit to Manning but was denied a confidential meeting. Private Manning's lawyers and thousands of supporters protested his treatment for months, but officials as high up as President Obama defended his treatment as status quo. Musicians Graham Nash and James Raymond wrote a song titled "Almost Gone," a phrase that Manning's lawyer used to describe his mental health after he had endured months of solitary confinement. A YouTube video of the song, comparing Manning to famous conscientious objectors, went viral (http://www.youtube.com/watch?v=dAYG7yJpBbQ).

The following commentary from a *New York Times* reader seemingly sums up the dual sentiments of many:

This guy acted according to his conscience but his judgment was definitely flawed, and he will be convicted and punished for it. He violated an oath but I think calling him a traitor and simply claiming that all secrets should be held equally deserving of confidentiality is also a flawed notion.

The anger that some people feel towards a "snitch" reveals a primitive urge to belong to a group and to justify even the egregious acts committed by group members. When soldiers murdered and raped civilians in a village that supported

Communist forces in Vietnam under orders, a helicopter crew rescued some of the villagers. It took decades for the DOD [Department of Defense] to cite those crew members for bravery and many in the military and amongst American civilians vilified them as traitors. The officers in charge of the troops were tried and either acquitted by military courts, never prosecuted, or pardoned by the President. There were soldiers who refused to participate who did not care what . . . the consequences [were. They] and this helicopter crew [were heroes]. . . . nobody else . . . [was] capable of doing the right thing. . . . Everyone else was just going along to get along.

Casual Observer, Los Angeles (February 28, 2013)

IMPACT OF LEAKED INFORMATION

The Arab Spring (movements to oust oppressive governments and foster democracy in Tunisia, Libya, and Egypt, as well as other countries in the Middle East, beginning in December 2010) is in part linked to the cables that Manning sent to WikiLeaks for dissemination. The leaked cables exposed government corruption, such as one case in which the daughter of the president of Tunisia and her husband used government funds to fly their favorite ice cream into Tunisia from Saint-Tropez while most of their country's population lived in oppressive poverty. This scandal apparently played a role in triggering the suicide of Tarek al-Tayeb Mohamed Bouazizi, a Tunisian street vendor who set himself on fire in December 2010 to protest the confiscation of his wares and harassment by a municipal official and her aides. In response to the actions of Bouazizi and others involved in the Arab Spring, as well as protests against governments around the world, *Time* magazine named "the protester" its 2011 person of the year.

U.S. Navy Admiral Michael Mullen, then chairman of the Joint Chiefs of Staff, said the leaks linked to Manning had placed the lives of American soldiers and Afghan informants in danger (Jaffe and Partlow 2010). Defense Secretary Robert M. Gates also blasted WikiLeaks for putting lives in danger, pointing to leaked documents that included the names and villages of Afghan informants (Bumiller 2010). Pentagon spokesman Geoff Morrell labeled the leaked documents "a gift to terrorist organizations [that] . . . put at risk the lives of our troops" (Burns and Somaiya 2010). In a letter to WikiLeaks dated November 27, 2010, the State Department's legal adviser, Harold Koh, said that the release of names

could place at risk the lives of countless innocent individuals—from journalists to human rights activists and bloggers to soldiers to individuals providing information to further peace and security. . . . Despite your stated desire to protect those lives, you have done the opposite and endangered the lives of countless individuals. You have undermined your stated objective by disseminating this material widely, without redaction, and without regard to the security and sanctity of the lives your actions endanger.

Assange countered that the documents "constituted the most comprehensive and detailed account of any war ever to have entered the public record" and showed that "Iraq was a bloodbath on every corner" (Burns and Somaiya 2010). He argued that WikiLeaks had done the world an immense service by documenting 15,000 previously unknown civilian deaths in Iraq. This put the human cost of the war in Iraq five times higher than that of the war in Afghanistan, Assange said, a previously hidden fact.

It is difficult to estimate how many people died as a result of Bradley Manning's alleged leaking of government documents. The first group of documents that WikiLeaks released, in the summer of 2010, very explicitly named secret informants. In October 2010, WikiLeaks released a second group of documents that had to do with the Iraq war; in these documents, names of specific individuals were omitted.

By May 2012, concrete evidence of deaths linked to the leaked documents began to emerge. An example is the hanging death of Western spy Majid Jamali Fashi in Tehran after he "confessed" to assassinating a nuclear scientist on behalf of Israel, according to a British media report (Ser 2012). The *Times* of London reported that a September 2009 document from the U.S. embassy in Baku, Azerbaijan, called attention to Fashi. That diplomatic document quotes an Iranian source who was a licensed martial arts coach and trainer as describing to his American contacts pressure from the Iranian regime to train soldiers and militiamen in martial arts. Fashi had been in Baku for an international martial arts competition only days before the U.S. embassy document was written. The suggestion was that the Iranian authorities identified Fashi as someone who was in illegal contact with the West on the basis of the document. He was arrested days after the publication of the document by WikiLeaks in December 2010 and charged with carrying out the January 2010 assassination of nuclear scientist Masoud Ali-Mohammadi on behalf of Mossad, Israel's national intelligence agency.

The British website Anorak (which describes itself as "an independent online sensation exposing prejudice, inhumanity, stuff shirts, misogyny, a biased news agenda, conformity, misanthropy, spin and the worst and best of human culture in words, pictures and video") described thousands of lives put in jeopardy by the documents Manning turned over to WikiLeaks:

> WikiLeaks has killed 1,300 people. OK, not killed but led to their deaths. Not our opinion but that of fame-hungry Julian Assange, who has undone the brilliant site by steering it towards an anti-USA agenda and media prominence. He claims that WikiLeaks swung the Kenyan 2007 elections. There was much bloodshed:
>
> > *"1,300 people were eventually killed, and 350,000 were displaced. That was a result of our leak."*

Well . . .

> *"On the other hand, the Kenyan people had a right to that information and 40,000 children a year die of malaria in Kenya. And many more die of money being pulled out of Kenya, and as a result of the Kenyan shilling being debased."*

Spoken like a true hard-nosed capitalist. As he said:

> *"WikiLeaks is designed to make capitalism more free and ethical."*

The dead will doubtless salute the ideal. . . . (http://www.Anorak.co .uk/267106/politicians/wikileaks-killed-1300-people-and-counting.html, December 3, 2010)

A week later Assange denied the comment and said, "Not a single person, as far as anyone is aware, has been harmed [by WikiLeaks]" (http://www.anorak.co .uk/267577/news/julian-assange-says-wikileaks-killed-1300-kenyans-then-denies-it.html, December 8, 2010).

CHARGES ARE FILED; MANNING PLEADS GUILTY TO TEN COUNTS

The U.S. Army filed twenty-two charges against Manning (see Box 5.2). On February 28, 2013, Manning pled guilty to ten of the twenty-two charges, which would yield a minimum twenty-year prison sentence. He refused to plead guilty to "aiding the enemy," which could carry a life sentence.

Box 5.2 Charges Filed Against Bradley Manning by the U.S. Army

---

- One count of "Aiding the enemy"
- Nine counts of "Failure to obey a lawful order or regulation"
  - o Transferring classified information to nonsecure systems
  - o Modifying or installing unauthorized software to a system and using it for unintended purposes.
  - o Circumventing security mechanisms
  - o Improper storage of classified information

- Twenty-four counts of violating various sections of the U.S. Code:
  - o Embezzlement and Theft of Public Money, Property or Records
  - o The Espionage Act: taking national defense information and either retaining it or delivering it to persons not entitled to receive it
  - o The Computer Fraud and Abuse Act

Manning admitted in court that he provided archives of military and diplomatic files to WikiLeaks. He pled guilty to ten criminal counts in connection with the material he leaked, which included the videos of air strikes in Iraq and Afghanistan in which civilians were killed, the logs of military incident reports, assessment files of detainees held at Guantánamo Bay, Cuba, and the 251,000 cables from American diplomats stationed around the world. He read a statement describing how he joined the military, became an intelligence analyst in Iraq, decided that certain files should become known to the American public to prompt a wider debate about foreign policy, downloaded them from a secure computer network and then ultimately uploaded them to WikiLeaks.

Judge (Colonel) Denise Lind then asked Manning to explain how he could admit that his actions were wrong. Manning replied, "Your Honor, regardless of my opinion or my assessment of documents such as these, it's beyond my pay grade—it's not my authority to make these decisions about releasing confidential files" (Savage 2013). Manning said he put the files on a digital storage card for his camera and took it home with him on a leave in early 2010. He then decided to give the files to newspapers. He first called the *Washington Post,* but the reporter he spoke with rebuffed him. He then called the *New York Times* and left a voice mail message that was not returned. He then called the public line at Bloomberg News but received no response. It was then that he copied the files and uploaded them to WikiLeaks.

The Freedom of the Press Foundation, a nonprofit group "dedicated to supporting journalism that combats overreaching government secrecy," issued a statement expressing concern about the Manning trial:

> We have been disturbed that Manning's pre-trial hearings have been hampered by the kind of extreme government secrecy that his releases to WikiLeaks were intended to protest. While reporters are allowed in the courtroom, no audio or visual recordings are permitted by the judge, no transcripts of the proceedings or any motions by the prosecution have been released, and lengthy court orders read on the stand by the judge have not been published for public review. (Timm and Reitman 2013)

In a pretrial hearing similar to a grand jury procedure that precedes a general court-martial, Manning's lawyer persuaded the judge that Manning should have the opportunity to show that he did not know that in leaking the documents, he was indirectly providing them via the Internet to al-Qaeda. (Some of Manning's leaked documents were found on Osama bin Laden's computer.)

On July 30, 2013, Judge Lind found Manning guilty of 17 of the original 22 crimes he was charged with, including several violations of the Espionage Act. In addition, he was found guilty of 4 more amended charges. He was not, however, found guilty of the most serious charge, aiding the enemy, which his attorneys considered a huge victory. On August 21, 2013, Manning was sentenced to 35 years in prison.

EPILOGUE

I recently received the following anonymous e-mail, which offers an interesting counterbalance to the Bradley Manning guerrilla government story:

Dear Professor O'Leary,

> More than a year ago I was asked to accept a major role in an assignment which would have involved helping to move supporters of an anti-Iranian group from one location in Iraq to another. At the time the group was classified as a foreign terrorist organization by the U.S. government. It is important to note that at the outset my personal perspective on international politics was neither pro nor anti-Iranian. I opposed taking the assignment on principle, which I will explain further.
>
> Professor O'Leary, I was under considerable pressure at the time by my superiors to accept this assignment. My viewpoint had not arisen out of the blue. Rather, I had already spent roughly three weeks with the group in question and this had given me plenty of time to understand its political philosophy. I felt that the framework of the group's motivations was rather weak and supported more by a large war chest and a well-oiled publicity machine.
>
> Professor O'Leary, I chose to decline the assignment after disagreeing very strongly with my immediate superior. He then took my decision to a second superior to explain my opposition to the assignment. This individual then asked me subsequently why I had vehemently declined the assignment. He doubted the logic of my explanation but eventually accepted my standpoint. I explained to this superior officer that my personal opposition to the group in question would compromise the integrity of the mission, i.e., their transfer from one location to another in Iraq. I explained further that I could not, in all fairness, accept the assignment given my personal stance. I believed that the group in question had cultish-like qualities and that any attempt to assist them did not enhance the status of our organization. Nor did it reflect the group's true nature. My opposition to this attempt to press me into leading this project was perhaps the most difficult decision of my career. To this day, I believe that this dissent was based on a principled set of arguments which I could not compromise on and would not change, even though I felt considerable pressure.
>
> The incident represented a valuable lesson to me in that it was one of the first times in my career where taking a principled stand against two superiors did not result in any immediate punitive measures against me. It was a very hard decision, but the right one and the dissent was the cornerstone of my motivation and actions.

6

Managing Guerrilla Government: Ethical Crusaders or Insubordinate Renegades?

TAKEN AS A WHOLE, the stories of guerrilla government profiled in this book illustrate several common themes concerning the power of career public servants that cross policy and temporal lines. The themes also bring together implications for public policy, public management, ethics, and governance. The major themes represented in these cases and others like them can be categorized into different types of harsh realities, discussion of which has generally been absent in the literature to date. After probing these harsh realities, I will close this chapter by presenting advice offered by "the pros" concerning how to manage dissent.

HARSH REALITIES OF GUERRILLA GOVERNMENT

Harsh Reality 1: Guerrilla government is here to stay.

Ask any seasoned, long-term public servants if guerrilla government exists, and their answer is likely to be "It happens." Ask them whether it is a good or a bad thing, and their answer will probably be "It depends." They then are apt to launch into stories (Maynard-Moody and Musheno 2003) that communicate their wonder, disgust, or something in between at the guerrilla government episodes they have personally experienced or heard about.

Whether seen as good or bad, the potential role of government guerrillas in influencing policy and programs is immense. The episodes highlighted in this book capture the actions of, and the methods used by, career public servants to affect the policies and programs of their bureaucracies from outside their organizations. These episodes present a useful contrast to the stereotype of the government bureaucrat interested only in a stable job, few risks, and a dependable retirement. Stillman (2004), for example, describes the common view of career public servants as "essentially the 'doing' and 'implementing' functionaries of bureaucracy" (153) who are "removed from the public" (189): soldiers on the front line with a "head-down attitude." While Stillman's description may fit some career bureaucrats, the truth is that this is a Swiss cheese stereotype—one riddled with holes.

As the bureaucratic politics literature overviewed in chapter 1 so aptly communicates, for better or for worse, bureaucrats and bureaucracies—whether the local post office, the state division of motor vehicles, or the Congressional Budget Office—are driven by their own highly particularized and parochial views, interests, and values (Long 1949). They are endowed with certain resources, including expertise (Benveniste 1977; Lewis 1988), longevity, insider information, contacts, and responsibility (Rourke 1984). They co-opt and will continue to seek to co-opt outside groups as a means of averting threats (Selznick 2011). This is a fact of life in the open systems and open organizations of public management. While the intensity of guerrilla government activities will ebb and flow, guerrilla government itself will never completely disappear.

Harsh Reality 2: Guerrillas can do it to you in ways you'll never know.

Based on the episodes highlighted in this book, as well as interviews with other career public servants, Box 6.1 presents an overview of guidelines for guerrillas from guerrillas—methods utilized by dissatisfied public servants to address perceived wrongs and to influence their organizations' policies. These range from putting a work order at the bottom of the desk drawer and forgetting about it to slipping information to a legislative staff person to outright insubordination. Some of these are strategies that the managers of the guerrillas must be aware of, whereas others are completely hidden from view. Realistically, absent hiring a full-time private detective, public managers need to realize that they will always have limited knowledge about, and control over, the career public servants in their organizations.

Box 6.1 Guidelines for Guerrillas from Guerrillas

---

1. Confront the issue directly with the person involved.
2. Talk to your supervisor.
3. Go over your supervisor's head—talk to your supervisor's supervisor.
4. Contact headquarters.
5. File a lawsuit.
6. Obey your superiors in public, but disobey them in private.

 7. Leak information.
 8. Create, or arrange for the creation of, documentaries, scientific studies, and scientific papers to describe and analyze the situation that concerns you.
 9. Cultivate positive relationships with interest groups.
10. Forge links with other outside groups: other professionals, nongovernmental organizations, concerned citizens.
11. Build public-private partnerships.
12. Build partnerships among entities at all levels of government.
13. Ghostwrite letters, testimony, and studies for supportive interest groups.
14. Lobby for your cause (and perhaps against your agency).
15. Testify before a legislative body.
16. Cultivate members of Congress and other elected officials, as well as their staff, as allies.
17. Contact a friend of a friend who works in the White House (or for any other elected official).
18. Write to the president of the United States.
19. Fail to correct superiors' mistakes: let them fall.
20. Neglect policies and directives you disagree with—stall.
21. Fail to implement orders you think are unfair.
22. Use a National Academy of Sciences review panel or similar independent panel of experts to force scientific attention to the problem.
23. File a complaint with the Office of the Inspector General.
24. Hold clandestine meetings to plot a unified staff strategy.
25. Tie your cause to a national or regional crisis, cause, or movement.
26. Raise your own funds for your cause.
27. Directly and openly blast the head of the agency.
28. Arrange for, or go along with, a transfer to another office.
29. Refuse to go along with a transfer to another office.
30. Quit.

Professionalized bureaucrats dominate information creation, analysis, and transmission, giving them a capacity to structure and suppress alternatives and premises (Lewis 1988). The alternatives from among which politicians and political appointees choose particular actions usually are drawn up by career public servants, who naturally build in their own professional biases and desires (Milward 1980). It is difficult for a political appointee manager to know what he or she is getting in the way of analyses from these experts, who are simultaneously claimants on scarce public resources. As one public manager put it:

They can do it to you in ways that you'll never know. [Career public servants] . . . can give you less than their best effort and it's hard to tell. Or in the worst case, if they were angry enough, they could set you up. They are very smart people—you don't want to fool with them. You need to treat them with respect in a participatory way. (O'Leary, Durant, Fiorino, and Weiland 1999, 274)

Another public manager opined:

Staff have figured out that if they don't like the decision the manager makes, they can go to the press, or Congress, or to an . . . interest group. When that happens, you've got a real big problem. If you take the position that you are going to take on an issue that is contrary to staff recommendations, you damn well better go in and explain it with them in depth before you make the decision. Otherwise you are going to find yourself defending your decision in the press or at a congressional hearing. (O'Leary et al. 1999, 274)

Still a third manager put it this way:

I've seen a number of managers get into trouble by blowing off staff concerns and not being willing to debate the issues with them. . . . Generally they will accept the reality of making political accommodations on occasion as long as you don't get too cavalier with the facts. The important thing is you've got to be willing to sit down with them and . . . explain your decisions to them. (O'Leary et al. 1999, 273–274)

Otherwise you may be in big trouble.

Harsh Reality 3: All guerrilla activity is not created equal.

How does one know whether a government guerrilla is a canary in a coal mine that needs to be listened to or a delusional single-issue fanatic? We all know the negative stories of guerrillas within metropolitan police departments whose views of policing are at odds with their departments' policies, but who believe they are promoting the public interest in crime control. And the differences between the Claude Fergusons and the Oliver Norths of the world seem fairly obvious.

And then there are the nuts or the "misguided." One self-labeled guerrilla sent me his entire personnel file, which measured over a foot high. He is a persecuted guerrilla, he wrote, and it all started when a consultant bought him a five-dollar hamburger at McDonald's and refused reimbursement. The employee reported the incident to his superior, citing ethics rules that mandate arms-length relationships between consultants and state employees. His superior advised him to forget it, as it was only a five-dollar hamburger and they had more important things to do with their time. Incensed, the employee filed a complaint against his superior and waged a clandestine war to get the consultant barred from future state contracts and his superior fired. His personnel file documents that he eventually filed seven separate complaints against seven separate superiors, working his way up the chain of command. When asked why he did what he did, he responded that he wanted to "do the right thing."

It is easy to laugh at a guerrilla who wages an all-out war over a five-dollar hamburger. But most cases are not so easy to judge. It is often difficult to sort out the "ethical" guerrillas from the "unethical" guerrillas, the guided from the misguided. For example, what or who, exactly, is "the public" in these instances? Possible "masters" a public servant might have include the public as interest group, the public as consumer (of government products), the public as elected representative, the public as client (served by "street-level bureaucrats"), and the public as citizen (Frederickson 1991). Claude Ferguson's competing obligations (Box 4.1) as well as the letters written against and in favor of his actions (Boxes 4.3 and 4.4) demonstrate the complexity of such cases.

Even when the outcome of guerrilla government activity is beneficial, the ethics of guerrilla government actions can be difficult to sort out. Did the government guerrillas profiled in this book act in a manner that can be deemed accountable and responsive to the public? Yes and no. All government organizations are to implement the will of the people as mandated by legislation enacted by elected representatives. Yet in the Nevada Four episode, for example, by not being constrained by the prevailing DOI and NDOW interpretations of congressional and state will and promoting new wetlands legislation, the Nevada Four promoted innovative policies that in the end also must be seen as the will of the people, since they eventually were enacted by Congress and approved by the people of Nevada in a referendum. Both sets of legislation were supported by the public: interest groups, consumers, elected representatives, clients, and citizens. At the same time, both sets of legislation were opposed by differing factions of the same public. Similarly, the Seattle EPA staff were there to serve the public interest, but they also were there to serve the regional administrator against whom they fought. In the same fashion, concerned citizens wrote letters to newspapers both condemning and praising Claude Ferguson.

The WikiLeaks scandal is even more challenging to sort out. Many say that Bradley Manning was a traitor to his country and there is no conceivable reason he needed to leak hundreds of thousands of documents, some of which ended up in the hands of terrorists and can be traced to a loss of lives. Others see Manning as similar to a conscientious objector, righteously exposing the literally bloody truth about thousands of civilian murders by the U.S. military that had been covered up by the Pentagon.

Examining this phenomenon through the lens of Waldo's (1988) twelve competing ethical obligations, it is important to note that all of the guerrillas in these episodes clearly did not see their allegiance, accountability, and responsiveness to their organizations as their first priority. Kipling's poem "If" (see Box 4.5) illustrates that Claude Ferguson's main obligation was to himself. In fact, the comments of all the guerrillas profiled here make it clear that they considered organizational pressures to be barriers to their "doing the right thing." As one scholar maintains, too little emphasis has been placed on understanding the important dimensions of public employee ethics in organizational settings (Denhardt 1988).

The paradox of this situation can be seen in the fact that the Nevada Four felt they had to "embarrass the government" to achieve their goals, when they themselves were, of course, the government. The Seattle EPA staff felt they had to do an end run around the government, yet they were the government. Claude Ferguson had to sue the government, when he was in fact part of the government. Bradley Manning felt that he needed to expose the atrocities of war inflicted by the U.S. government, yet, as a member of the U.S. Army, he was part of that government. In the end, these guerrillas' commitments were not to their organizations or to the public as interest group, the public as consumer, the public as elected representative, the public as client, or the public as citizen. Rather, their commitments were to their own personal interpretations of the public interest, profession and professionalism, self, perhaps even to nation, humanity, and, for some, God.

Who Defines What Is Ethical?

The issue then becomes, Whose ethics? Two different scholars of ethics have written that ethical behavior on behalf of a public official means acting with integrity. Fleishman (1981) defines integrity as follows:

> Simply put, "integrity" means having a genuine, wholehearted disposition to do the right and just thing in all circumstances, and to shape one's actions accordingly. There is no code of conduct declaring society's view of the right course of action in every situation, so each of us must puzzle out for ourselves the moral solution to each dilemma we face. (53)

Dobel (1999) defines integrity as

> a balance among the three domains of personal moral commitments and capacities, obligations of office, and political prudence. It depends upon self-conscious reflection, honesty, and the self-disciplined ability to resist temptation and act upon beliefs and commitments. Possessing integrity obligates individuals to know and address the legal, moral, and practical dimensions of an issue in making their decisions. (213)

Based on these definitions and the definitions provided in chapter 1, did the guerrillas profiled in the episodes presented in this book act with integrity, responsibility, and ethics? Yes and no. Assuming that they had a wholehearted disposition to do the right and just thing in all circumstances, made their decisions based on self-conscious reflection, honesty, and a resistance to temptation, and acted upon their beliefs and commitments, the answer is yes. Yet many actions of individual guerrillas crossed the line to unethical behavior. An example is the Nevada Four inviting a senator to tour the refuge and then telling their superiors that he had requested the tour. Clearly this was crossing the line. Implying that selenium toxicosis might be the cause of the massive fish kill without having fully analyzed the issue was unprofessional at best, unethical at worst. Manning's exposing Afghan informants and putting their lives in danger could easily be seen as unethical.

To some, however, the guerrillas' actions are examples of brilliant entrepreneurship (Doig and Hargrove 1987; Riccucci 1995). In the eyes of particular interest groups, consumers, clients, and citizens, some guerrillas are heroic bureaucrats (Couto 1991). Some are seen as policy entrepreneurs, as illuminated by Lewis (1980) and Kingdon (2010). A member of the Sierra Club touted the Nevada Four's actions as the highest service to our country. Claude Ferguson won many national environmental awards for his actions. The displaced director of management in the Seattle regional office of the EPA eventually was promoted to the Senior Executive Service and made deputy regional administrator. Activist Daniel Ellsberg praised Bradley Manning as a hero.

To others, however, the actions of some of the guerrillas constitute outrageous insubordination. While Ferguson received many letters of support, he and the local newspapers received numerous letters from citizens who were aghast that he would assertively argue for what they perceived to be his own policy preferences (see Boxes 4.3 and 4.4). To some, the career public servants in the EPA's Seattle regional office during the Reagan administration were the embodiment of stubborn and misguided institutionalization: long-timers who represented a culture different from that of the new political leaders voted in by the American people. Some believe that Manning deserves to be court-martialed and imprisoned for life for betraying his country. It is indeed a part of the paradox that this same "deviant" behavior of the guerrillas can be looked at as the savvy use of public management tools, such as the cultivation of the press and alliances with interest groups.

But suppose these guerrillas were anti-Black, anti-Muslim skinheads who used these tools to undermine federal civil rights actions? What if they were religious-right fundamentalists dedicated to halting the teaching of evolution in public schools? Obviously, in such cases guerrillas' shrewd use of the same public management tools would most likely be seen as manipulative, troublesome, and, to most, unethical. In fact, one of the Nevada Four who reviewed a draft of this book expressed a fear that it could become "guidance to midlevel bureaucrats whose political motivation and personal ambition exceed ethical and legal standards and requirements" (correspondence with author, 2004).

The stories of guerrilla government told in this book are examples of what one scholar of administrative ethics calls "the problem of ambiguity" (Rohr 1989). These government guerrillas, like most public servants, have many masters, competing ethical obligations, and multiple directions of accountability. To some they are brilliant entrepreneurs. To others they are deviant insubordinates.

What can we take, then, from these episodes in the way of ethical insight? At the very least, important questions emerge that potential government guerrillas should ask themselves before they decide to go the guerrilla government route. Every potential guerrilla should ask him- or herself the following questions:

1. Am I correct? More than a sincere belief is needed.
2. Is the feared damage immediate, permanent, and irreversible? Are safety and health issues involved? Or is there time for a longer view and a more open strategy?
3. Am I adhering to the rule of law?
4. Is there a legitimate conflict of laws?
5. Is this an area that is purely and legitimately discretionary?
6. Have all reasonable alternative avenues been pursued?
7. Would it be more ethical to dissent publicly to my supervisor?
8. Would it be more ethical to promote transparency rather than work clandestinely?
9. Would it be more ethical to work with sympathetic legislators before turning to media and outside groups?
10. Is public whistle-blowing a preferable route?

This will remain a difficult area of public management to sort out. It is a fact that all guerrilla activity is not created equal. How a public manager decides which behavior is legitimate and which crosses unacceptable boundaries could be the most important question of that individual's career.

Harsh Reality 4: Most public organizations are inadequately equipped to deal effectively with guerrilla government.

As seen in these episodes, there are at least four primary conditions that tend to yield situations that encourage the festering of guerrilla government activities. These may occur alone or in combination:

1. When internal opportunities for voicing one's dissent are limited or decline
2. When the perceived cost of voicing one's opposition is greater than the perceived cost of engaging in guerrilla government activities
3. When the issues involved are personalized or the subject of deeply held values
4. When quitting one's job or leaving one's agency is seen as having a destructive (rather than salutary) effect on the policies of concern

Some of these conditions can be addressed through the application of key ideas found in conflict resolution theory. The conflict resolution literature asks whether there is an alterative avenue—perhaps an internal organizational channel—available through which government guerrillas can be brought back into their organizations, despite their inherent mistrust of regular channels (Brower and Abolafia 1997). Is there a way to channel their energy for the common good? Is there a way to resolve small conflicts before they escalate into guerrilla warfare?

Contrasted to the idea of Hirschman (1970) and his followers that the four primary options available to disgruntled employees are exit, voice, loyalty, and neglect, the conflict resolution literature offers its own view of four options available to disillusioned employees: avoidance, collaboration, higher authority, and unilateral power play (Slaikeu and Hasson 1998). "Avoidance" means no action is taken to resolve the conflict. "Collaboration" can be an individual initiative, negotiation among the parties themselves, or mediation by a third party. "Higher authority" is referral up the line of supervision or chain of command, internal appeals, formal investigation, or litigation. "Unilateral power play" can include behind-the-scenes maneuvering, physical violence, or strikes. The guerrilla government approach examined in this study is a combination of collaboration, unilateral power play, and higher authority.

In this context, *problem solving* may be a better term to use in the public sector than *conflict resolution,* because conflicts—especially public bureaucratic conflicts—are not contests to be won but rather shared problems to be solved (Ury, Brett, and Goldberg 1993). Moreover, public bureaucratic conflicts need to be dealt with at the earliest possible point in time. Carpenter and Kennedy (2001) discuss the "spiral of unmanaged conflict" (11) that begins when one or more parties choose not to acknowledge that a problem exists. Activities escalate as groups attempt to gain recognition for their concerns, and eventually more effort, time, and money are devoted to winning than to solving the problem. As a conflict rises up, the spiral becomes something like a tornado, with sides forming, positions hardening, communication stopping, and perceptions becoming distorted. Eventually the dispute goes beyond the program, and perhaps beyond the organization. The press may get involved, a legislative body may become involved, and, in the worst cases, all-out war may be declared. The lesson of the spiral is not that it is inevitable, but that it is predictable if nothing is done to address the conflict.

Any sort of short-term effort to address guerrilla government challenges must be combined with long-term designs to transform the entire conflict system of an organization by addressing its structural roots. This has been called an "underdog" approach rather than the conventional "top dog" orientation (Costantino and Merchant 1996). It embraces prevention and avoidance as well as resolution and settlement.

"Dispute system design" is a phrase coined by Ury et al. (1993) to describe an organization's effort to diagnose and improve the way it manages conflict. A systems approach to dispute system design, which identifies those subsystems that make up the whole and examines how well they collectively interact in order to discover how to improve them, is important. Much of this branch of conflict resolution theory builds on the work of the open systems theorists profiled in chapter 1, who viewed organizations as open—not closed. Parts of organizations are dynamically interrelated with each other and with entities in their environment. Open systems thinking encourages an emphasis on the whole and the interaction of the parts, not on the parts themselves. In addition, open systems thinking requires the organization to be responsive to external changes.

Only in the past twenty years have large organizations, especially large public organizations, begun to create conflict management systems. It is a relatively new idea that an organization's conflict management system is intricately involved in the effectiveness of the entire organization. Many early attempts at creating conflict management systems in organizations yielded offices that were walled off from the rest of their organizations, such as legal offices and personnel offices. One envisions a lonely office door labeled "Dissenters Enter Here."

In 2001, the Society of Professionals in Dispute Resolution (now the Association for Conflict Resolution) combined the best practices in this area to form recommendations for integrated conflict management system design. These include encouraging employees and managers (such as the guerrillas profiled here) to voice concerns and constructive dissent early, integrating collaborative problem-solving approaches into the culture of the organization, encouraging direct negotiation among the parties in a dispute, and aligning conflict management practices with each other and with the mission, vision, and values of the organization. Many of these suggestions are amazingly close to the advice given by the professional managers I interviewed, which is presented in the last half of this chapter. From this work come five essential characteristics of integrated conflict management systems that, while dated, still are applicable and relevant to guerrilla government today:

1. Options for addressing all types of problems are available to all people in the workplace, including employees, supervisors, professionals, and managers.
2. A culture that welcomes dissent and encourages resolution of conflict at the lowest level through direct negotiation is created.
3. Multiple access points and persons who are easily identified as knowledgeable and trustworthy for approaching with advice about a conflict or the system are provided. Examples include ombudsmen who help parties find ways to work within the system and experts who coach employees and managers regarding collaborative methods.
4. Multiple options for addressing conflicts, including rights-based (such as when legal or contractual rights have been violated) and interest-based (such as negotiation and mediation) processes exist.
5. A systemic structure that coordinates and supports the multiple access points and multiple options and integrates effective conflict management practices into daily organizational operations is provided. (Society of Professionals in Dispute Resolution 2001)

The point is to create and promote a workplace climate in which disputes are constructively addressed and resolved. Our public organizations need to learn how to tap into the potentially insightful, creative ideas and energy of dissenters in order to make constructive changes in their systems when appropriate.

This is in keeping with much of the literature in organization theory and management. Slater and Bennis (1990), for example, espouse more democratic organizations that have the following characteristics:

- Full and free communication, regardless of rank and power
- A reliance on consensus, rather than the more customary forms of coercion or compromise, to manage conflict
- The idea that influence is based on technical competence and knowledge rather than on the vagaries of personal whims or prerogatives of power
- An atmosphere that permits and even encourages emotional expression as well as task-oriented acts
- A basically human bias, one that accepts the inevitability of conflict between the organization and the individual and is willing to cope with and mediate this conflict on rational grounds

This is one of the few areas of public management where the literature and theory are ahead of the day-to-day practice. There is a need for sweeping reform of public organizations concerning institutional processes and procedures for dealing with angry dissenters. Only when such reform has taken place will we see the instances of guerrilla government decrease.

Harsh Reality 5: The tensions inherent in guerrilla government will never be resolved.

The dilemma of guerrilla government is truly a public policy paradox: there is a need for accountability and control in our government organizations, but that same accountability and control can stifle innovation and positive change. Put another way, there is a need in government for career bureaucrats who are policy innovators and risk takers, but at the same time there is a need for career bureaucrats who are policy sustainers. Hence the actions of the government guerrillas studied in this book are manifestations of the complex environment in which our public managers function, and every public manager needs to be aware of this.

Inherent in this paradox are many perennial clashing public management tensions and issues. These tensions include the need for control versus the perceived need to disobey, the need for hierarchy versus the need for local autonomy, and built-in tensions in the organizational structures and missions of organizations themselves. Further: To whom are these career public servants accountable? To whom are they to be responsive? Whose ethical standards are they to follow to gauge whether their own behaviors are responsible?

Embedded in the cornerstones of public management are the concepts of hierarchical control and accountability. In the case of a large bureaucracy such as the U.S. Army, the Department of Agriculture, the Department of the Interior, or the Environmental Protection Agency, or even a small state or local agency with a meager staff, it would be difficult to argue that there is not a valid need for control of employees and obedience to the policies and procedures dictated from the top of the organization. If all employees in such an organization actively disobeyed orders and made policy decisions based on their own personal agendas and interests, no matter how heartfelt, chaos would reign and the organization might fail to exist as a coherent whole. The public interest clearly would not be served.

At the same time, even if we acknowledge the potential dark side to guerrilla government (see, e.g., Adams and Balfour 2009), it is clear that the major force driving all of the career bureaucrats studied in this book was neither disobedience for the sake of disobedience nor pure self-interest. Rather, all of them expressed being driven by outrage at the perceived actual or potential harm caused by their organizations' policies. All expressed being driven by a personal sense of what is right.

Just as it is difficult to argue that there is not a need for obedience by employees, it is difficult to argue *overall* that acting on one's strongly held personal and spiritual beliefs *in certain contexts* is improper. In fact, if there is a violation of the U.S. Constitution involved, at least one court has held that an employee has a right to disobey the policies in question. In *Harley v. Schuylkill County* (476 F. Supp. 191, 1979), which is still good law today, a Pennsylvania court held that the right to refuse to violate another's federal constitutional rights was a right secured by the Constitution. But since there apparently were no violations of constitutional rights involved in the episodes presented in this book, the world is fuzzier and the paradox and tensions remain.

Thus, on one hand, the career public servants who practice guerrilla government techniques may be seen as refreshing entrepreneurial winds of change in the tradition of those profiled in Doig and Hargrove's (1987) collection—activist, caring public servants with a personal commitment to protecting the environment. The Nevada Four's idea to seek donations of water rights for the wetlands, for example, changed the rules of the game and opened up a new world of policy options. On the other hand, government guerrillas may be seen as threats to accountability, control, and hierarchy, since they take actions against the wishes of their superiors. There is a need for employees who are committed personally to the policy issues affecting or affected by an organization; at the same time, there is a need for unified policy direction and action as well as for standard operating procedures. In addition, as Kaufman points out in *The Forest Ranger* (1960), there is, at times, a need for hierarchy to counterbalance possible co-optation of public servants by local communities. These tensions can never be fully resolved.

Complicating the issue, however, is the fact, as stated by a Washington, D.C., superior of one of the guerrillas profiled here, that the ideas and desires of the guerrillas most likely never would have been implemented had the guerrillas continued to work solely through their own bureaucracies. The reasons are threefold. First, the contrary and competing missions of most public organizations yield a situation where most major policy decisions are compromises. As Lewis (1988, 162) points out, high-level attention to a particular problem or issue typically is scarce, and prolonged consideration of a singular policy area is rare. Contrasted to this are the "prolonged attention subsystems" of professional bureaucrats that give them the capacity to initiate, fixate, and innovate (169). This is the status quo in most public organizations. While the airing of disparate views may be encouraged, for political reasons most public servants almost never totally obtain what they desire in terms of programmatic changes and resources. The tension here is between the realistic need for compromise in a large bureaucracy and the capacity of bureaucrats to initiate and innovate, which is unequaled in the U.S. political system.

Second, tied in with this are the sometimes-competing missions within the suborganizations themselves (Downs 1993). In the Fish and Wildlife Service, for example, the tasks of protecting endangered species and saving wetlands sometimes pull the organization in different directions, with the wetlands tending to get short shrift. Similarly, the Forest Service has the authority to manage the national forests for recreation, grazing, wildlife, fisheries, and wilderness preservation, in addition to timber and watershed purposes.

Third, the guerrillas would never have had the power bases inside their organizations that they were able to establish outside their organizations. By reaching out beyond their organizational boundaries and creating networks, the guerrillas expanded their power bases and possible routes to success.

How can these different views of "correct" public servant behavior be reconciled? How can these government guerrillas simultaneously be dedicated employees and not comply with the norms so carefully laid out by their organizations? How can we absorb the government guerrillas of the world into our vision of public organizations without merely dismissing these public servants as aberrations, radicals, outliers, or zealous nuts?

One clue lies in the work of David E. Mason, who studies nonprofit organizations and management and writes about the expressive behavior of employees. Many of Mason's ideas are applicable to public servants. As Mason (1996) defines it, expressive behavior is "action for direct rather than for indirect gratification" (xi); it fosters "activity for its own sake, looking only to itself for justification: participation for the sake of participation; work for the sake of work" (2). Contrasted to expressive behavior is instrumental behavior, which entails producing an output that is external to the organization. An action can be both instrumental to an organization (e.g., timber management) and expressive to an individual (e.g., protecting the environment). An action can also be instrumental to an individual (e.g., earning a paycheck) while simultaneously being expressive to that same individual (e.g., bonding with fellow workers). While there is nothing new about organizations fulfilling both expressive and instrumental needs, or individuals working for both instrumental and expressive purposes, it is safe to say that the leaders of most public programs give little attention to these issues in their organizations.

The environmental government guerrillas in the stories presented here acted for expressive, rather than instrumental, reasons. When a sense of integrity was the driving force, it was their own personal sense of integrity—not one manufactured by the organization—that took over. This is the expressive dimension. Yet managers—especially managers of public organizations—rarely want to discuss the expressive dimension of their organizations. They are encouraged, instead, to discuss options in terms of efficiency only, in terms of management only, in terms of budget only. While efficiency, management, and budget are of paramount importance, so too is the expressive dimension, which often manifests itself in issues of dissent, voice, and openness or lack of openness to new ideas.

While unbridled expressive behavior in an organizational context could lead to negative consequences, expressive activity *that is congruent with the core values of the organization* is important for several reasons. First, the opportunity for expressive activity attracts and motivates participants to work for instrumental purposes. Second, fulfilling the expressive needs of employees should yield better decision making as employees are made a legitimate part of the decision-making process. Third, expressive activity tends to encourage bottom-up communication, horizontal communication, and communication within the broad network of individuals interested in a certain policy domain. Finally, people need expressive activity as an end in itself.

The common view of public organizations is limited in that it often fails to accept or take into consideration the number of individuals who seek such employment opportunities for expressive as well as instrumental reasons (Perry, Hondeghem, and Wise 2010; Brewer, Selden, and Facer 2000). Examples include individuals who seek careers at NASA because they have deeply felt commitment to the future of spaceflight, individuals who seek careers in social welfare agencies because they want to alleviate poverty, and individuals who seek careers in state health departments because of a deep commitment to preventive health care practices. Simultaneously promoting expressive and instrumental objectives in our public agencies, when appropriate, is one step toward addressing the tensions inherent in guerrilla government. Taking that step will remain an important public management challenge for the leaders of those organizations.

ADVICE FROM THE PROS

As I was putting the finishing touches on the first edition of this book, my phone rang again. This time the call was from a government guerrilla named Doug Kerr, a conservation officer with the New York Department of Environmental Conservation. He, too, had heard about the book I was writing, and he had a story to tell. He showed up at my office the next week (in uniform, gun in holster) and allowed me to interview him for eight hours. Against the wishes of his superiors, he documented fraud and violation of environmental laws in the laying of the Iroquois natural gas pipeline from Canada to New York City in the 1990s. His tip to U.S. attorney yielded a lengthy lawsuit against the pipeline company that culminated in jail sentences for several company managers as well as one of the largest environmental fines in the history of the United States, second only to the fine paid by Exxon as a result of the *Exxon Valdez* oil spill off the coast of Alaska.

I followed up with interviews of the attorneys who won the case, an agent from the Federal Bureau of Investigation who investigated the pipeline company, and a concerned citizen who rallied other landowners against the pipeline company. All supported Doug Kerr's story in our lengthy interviews. Yet while not disputing the facts of Kerr's collection of evidence, tip, and unflagging commitment to the case, the attorneys and the FBI agent then dismissed the significance of Kerr's guerrilla activities. "Happens all the time," they told me. "Not that big a deal. Everyday bureaucratic activity."

Assuming, contrary to the views of the attorney and the detective, that guerrilla government activity is significant and should be a last (or near-last) resort of dissenters, what else might be done to reduce it, in addition to attention to dispute system design, organization dynamics, and integrating the expressive and instrumental objectives of organizations when appropriate? One possible answer lies in the training of new political appointees entering government for the first time at significant organization levels. A mandatory multiday training course is necessary, during which new appointees would learn about their own subordination to the rule of law, the constitutional requirements of their positions, the nature of legislative oversight, the desirability of working with career employees, and what it takes to lead in public agencies. As this book has demonstrated, guerrilla activity is sometimes promoted by foolish moves on the part of political appointees who think they have a mandate based on rhetoric uttered by a president while on the campaign trail and who think that career public administrators should be, and will be, the robotic implementers of the will of their superiors. Political appointees, as well as other high-level administrators, need to know that their capacity to destroy new ideas is as great as their capacity to create them. Each of the environmental episodes presented here shows how organizations can stifle good ideas and energy coming up from the staff. Ernesta Barnes in the Seattle EPA episode is a counterexample: she made a major difference, stemming guerrilla activity by actively embracing the guerrillas in her organization.

Of course, there will always be times when public managers will have to quash negative guerrilla government. Examples include, but are not limited to, when rights are in danger of being violated, laws are broken, or people may get hurt. Yet scholars who have studied empirically whether career public servants "work, shirk, or sabotage" have found that bureaucrats in the United States largely are highly principled, hardworking, responsive, and functioning (Brehm and Gates 1997, 195–202; see also Goodsell 2004; Feldman 1989; Wood and Waterman 1991, 1994; Golden 1992). Hence, when there are incidents of guerrilla government, managers need to view them as potentially serious messages that should be heard (Brower and Abolafia 1997).

Thus part of the training of political appointees, as well as other public managers, should be the communication of the conclusion that their first line of defense can no longer be dismissing government guerrillas as mere zealots or troublemakers. This perspective acknowledges the central importance of dissent in organizations.

I surveyed members of the National Academy of Public Administration (NAPA), an independent, nonpartisan organization chartered by Congress to assist federal, state, and local governments in improving their effectiveness, efficiency, and accountability; alumni of the Maxwell School of Syracuse University; and some of the veteran managers on the NASA Return to Flight Task Group I served on. I asked them about the value of dissent in organizations. Of the 216 current and former managers who responded, 213 indicated that dissent, when managed properly, is not only positive but also essential to a healthy organization. Box 6.2 contains a sampling of the comments from my respondents concerning the value of dissent in organizations and in our society as a whole.

Box 6.2 What Is the Value of Dissent in Organizations and to Society as a Whole?

"If managed properly, dissent can create an energy that can be cultivated for positive change or results within an organization."—*First deputy commissioner, New York City Taxi and Limousine Commission*

"In a technical organization, especially one where human lives are at risk, and that organization has the full responsibility for design, manufacturing, testing, and operation, dissent is an absolute essential element. Without it failure is assured."—*Former deputy director to Admiral Rickover, Nuclear Navy Program*

"Dissent allows the organization to define and get a grasp on the complexity of issues. Public organizations serve people with different interests, so there should be dissent/debate if the organization is keeping its mandate and really considering multiple viewpoints, especially concerning minority viewpoints and perspectives. Vulnerable populations do not have adequate representation, so public organizations often have responsibility to voice these issues in public realm."—*Program manager, U.S. Agency for International Development, Afghanistan*

"Dissent requires issues to be discussed, and often new information is discovered during this dialogue. Dissent also keeps projects, laws, etc. from being implemented in the heat of the moment. If managed well, dissenting individuals can also become enfranchised and envision a positive role for themselves in the government processes rather than sitting outside and throwing rocks."—*Former local government manager*

"The truth is best recognized by evaluating all perspectives."—*City attorney*

"Good 'followship' (the necessary parallel condition to good leadership), consist[s] of not only doing one's duty (i.e., what you are told), but also in helping keep 'the ship and its captain' on track. That requires dissenting from the vector leadership has taken. That dissent need not be destructive (as in mutiny); instead it must be in an organizational culture (fostered from the top) that actively solicits alternative views. To look reality squarely in the eye (as Jack Welch wrote) requires a selfless devotion to seeking what that truth is. Dissent is one important mechanism assuring that."—*Former manager, Department of Defense*

"It actually moves us further and faster when people are rigorously thinking about what the best decision is and the best way to get there. I would be concerned if there wasn't dissent."—*Managing director of recruitment, Teach for America*

"Dissent can be a constructive way to vet alternative views and the reasons for them that may lead to either honing of existing views or adjusting current positions or thinking if the evidence or logic so suggest. The dissent may also provide better insight into the size and intensity of the opposition."—*Senior fellow, Caliber Associates; former assistant secretary, planning and evaluation, U.S. Department of Health, Education, and Welfare; former assistant director, U.S. Office of Management and Budget; former deputy county executive, Fairfax County, Virginia*

"Dissent in an organization is healthy. A dissenting organization is like that of a healthy family. It is not perfect, quiet, reserved, or without its faults. It is at its best when it is functionally dysfunctional—a group of dynamic personalities thinking separately and working together as one. A healthy organization is not a group of people thinking as one and agreeing on everything but is one that disagrees often, loudly, and with devotion."—*Deputy center director, National Aeronautics and Space Administration*

(Continued)

Box 6.2 (Continued)

"Dissent yields better thinking about problems; better thinking in and among the bosses; higher levels of work satisfaction among more employees (I am heard); higher levels of ownership around decisions (I had input and they actually took my idea!); faster reaction to change of any sort (no mushroom theory); more trust and openness in conversations. Gets to problem solution faster; may be a better solution."—*Vice president for safety, BPI International*

"Dissent is important because it (1) results in different views being expressed, more openness, greater communication, higher-quality discourse, and broader thinking; (2) results in greater trust; (3) results in a more positive workplace that people want to be a part of; (4) results in people in the organization that are more committed to the mission and the leadership; (5) results in successful organizational outcomes."—*Director of research, Space Security Center*

"If there is no dissent in public organizations, then assumptions, theories, and proposed courses of action will not be rigorously thought through before critical strategic as well as tactical decisions are made. In my experience, the voices one learned to listen to most closely were those who had the courage to speak out in dissent to whatever consensus might be forming or to a preferred outcome that had been articulated by senior officials. Even if the eventual decision or direction was the same as it would have been without the dissent being voiced, the dissent served to force a reexamination of the logic, facts, and circumstances on which a consensus was being forged and thus, at the very minimum, made the basis for the decision stronger. Of course it is a guesstimate, but I would suggest that at least one-third of the time that there were strong, sustained, rigorous, and informed dissents, the decision or the direction was altered as a result."—*Former senior procurement executive, U.S. Department of the Interior*

"Dissent generates ideas that those in leadership positions may not have considered. It can also provide management with the 'pulse' of the organization."—*Contracting officer, U.S. Environmental Protection Agency*

"Dissent can bring the dynamic tension to organizations that is necessary to think clearly about all the positives and negatives of a course of action. It is critical to arriving at a well-thought-through decision."—*Public management consultant*

"Dissent can alert an organization to potential problems with its plans or direction. It can force leaders to a more careful assessment of their thinking and help them see problems they may not have anticipated. Smart leaders will create open channels that allow dissension to be expressed and its merits considered before dissenters are driven to take possibly harmful action."—*Director of credit programs for a large private university*

"Dissent, by definition, comes from below. Dissent from above is an order or direction. Dissent is a sign of a positive work environment and positive organizational empowerment. Maximization of each employee's potential within the framework of the organizational needs requires that employees be empowered to make decisions, solve problems, provide feedback, and, probably most importantly, dissent. Often, managers forget that the wheels of the organization are greased by the lower-echelon employees. These employees have insight into the logistics, administrative functioning, personnel issues, and corporate culture that managers, by definition, are not privy to. Dissent allows for these issues to be brought forward to the management team prior to poor decisions being made or bad policy being enacted."—*Litigation manager for a large federal agency*

"Dissent enables managers to learn about problems or misunderstandings that exist in the organization. These matters may relate to specific programs, personnel, or organization culture/structure. Dissent, if sensibly communicated and openly received, can lead to corrective action or, on occasion, fundamental change."—*Dean, school of public and international affairs*

"Embracing dissent means inviting diversity of opinion from the people around you," Sean O'Keefe, former administrator of NASA and now chairman and CEO of EADS North America, told me when we talked. "My first rule is to never surround myself with people who are just like me. My second rule is to always insist upon someone voicing the dissenting opinion. Always."

Thus, instead of discussing guerrillas as problematic and plotting how to get rid of them, we can think of a guerrilla as a messenger coming to tell a manager something important about the organization, its policies, and its way of operating. In the old days, if a king received a message he didn't like, he would sometimes have the messenger killed. This is denying the message or raging against it. The real challenge is to see if we can listen to government guerrillas' messages, sift through the canaries and the zealots, and really hear them and take what they say to heart—that is, make the connection to the broader reality of the public management and public policy challenges at hand.

Public managers need to use the opportunity of hearing guerrillas' messages to observe, be open, and learn, rather than jumping automatically into rejection and judging, thinking that they have somehow failed or that the organization is broken or does not work because dissent has been voiced. To the contrary, Kingdon (2010, 20) sees the "free-form process" triggered by bureaucratic entrepreneurs as promoting creativity and an opportunity for new and innovative ideas to emerge. These entrepreneurs act as brokers, negotiating among people, yielding couplings that might never have occurred in more structured settings.

Many managers look at organizations as machines, such as automobiles. A "problem" like guerrilla government happens, and it must be "fixed." Call in the consultants, find out who the guerrillas are, and make them go away by firing them, cutting them out of the process, or ostracizing them. Or worse, the consultants come up with some magic quick fix. But organizations are not machines, and guerrilla government is not just a "people problem." It is a set of inevitable tensions between bureaucracy and democracy and needs to be addressed in every organization.

The perspective of this book, then, is that some guerrillas just might be creative assets to the public organizations for which they work. Twenty years later, I'm glad I didn't "Fire the bastard!" But my boss wasn't totally misguided, for he clearly perceived the potential dark side of guerrilla government. Several of the respondents to my survey of managers pointed out the negatives of unbridled dissent. For example, Mitchel Wallerstein, president of Baruch College and an expert on national security issues, commented: "The negative aspects of dissent relate primarily to the corrosive effect they can have on the morale and discipline of an organization. In the national security world, dissent may be tolerated up to a point, but once an action is approved, additional dissent can upset carefully developed plans and, in extremis, can place people's lives in jeopardy." Dan Fiorino, former director of EPA National Environmental Performance Track and a NAPA member, said: "Often dissent that I have seen is the work of one or a few disgruntled employees who are using it to either give their lives meaning or to protect themselves against action for poor performance or behavior problems. It is an irritant to other people and may even damage morale." Other negative aspects of dissent mentioned by the leaders and managers who responded to my survey included the following: dissent can become a preoccupying force that distracts from the central mission of the organization; dissent can slow organization efficiency; dissent can lead to hurt feelings; dissent can be corrosive and destructive; and dissent can siphon off some of the organization's human capital to address whatever challenges the dissent may raise.

Given the potential negatives of dissent, is there a way that an organization can harness the creativity of guerrillas without engendering total chaos and allowing the dark side of guerrilla government to take over? In addition to the suggestions offered thus far in this book, the public managers I interviewed offered new insights, as detailed below. Many reinforce the suggestions mentioned earlier.[1]

Cultivate Organization Culture

Many of the managers who responded to my survey noted the importance of creating an organization culture that accepts, welcomes, and encourages candid dialogue and debate. They emphasized the need to cultivate a questioning attitude by encouraging staff to challenge the assumptions and actions of the organization.

The majority agreed that dissent, when managed well, can foster innovation and creativity. In particular, dissent can help generate multiple options that an organization might not normally consider. Managers should think of dissent as an opportunity to discuss alternative notions of how to achieve a goal. Cultivating the creative aspects behind dissent can lead to greater participation, higher job satisfaction, and ultimately better work product, the managers told me.

Organizations can avoid groupthink through diversity of thought and intellectual curiosity. Communicate that the staff can raise concerns without fear of retribution. Communicate that employees are expected and encouraged to offer innovative ideas to help solve problems. Communicate that differing opinions are welcome and respected. Send a clear message from the top that different points of view are valued. Acknowledge dissent and acknowledge that there is validity in the dissent. Communicate to all sides that they have been listened to.

A leader creates such a culture through what he or she says to employees, writes in newsletters and reports, communicates on the organization's website, and says in speeches; through the way he or she phrases goals, slogans, and mission statements; and, most important, through his or her actions on a daily basis. "Think of creating a positive organization culture the same way you think about raising a healthy, productive child from birth," wrote a retired organization psychologist. "Just as everything you say and do to a child counts from the day the child is born, so too does everything you say and do about an organization and people in that organization count every day that you are a leader."

Train supervisors to respond to employee questions in a measured, open, honest manner. Communicate that healthy conflict is a natural result of diversity of expertise and experience. Teach people to listen. Teach people to solve conflict. Be a consensus maker. Send a message that those who raise dissenting views, even if they ultimately do not change the outcome of the decision, will continue to be equally valued members of the team.

"Create an atmosphere where dissent is not seen as antagonistic or nonsupportive of the initiative being considered," suggested John Nalbandian, former mayor of Lawrence, Kansas, a professor at the University of Kansas, and a member of NAPA. "I wouldn't even call it dissent. Dissent implies revolution. Progress need not mean total revolt. Call it discussion." A NASA deputy center director put it another way:

> Open and clear dialogue is paramount for a productive dissent-based exchange of views and ideas. A healthy spirited debate that contests and challenges ideas and practices leads to a better understanding of their potential. It has to be a

fundamental principle of these discussions that once an idea has surfaced that the organization or group must hear and listen to it (hence, two ears and one mouth) and deal with it responsibly and respectfully.

An assistant town manager advised, "Clearly communicate that you are receptive to input from all employees, thereby improving communication and participation in decision making. Then follow through and do it." But "don't forget that above all else you are a leader," said another seasoned manager:

> Leadership is often confused with micromanaging in a very directive fashion. Organizations seem less tolerant of dissent than in past years. An example is Donald Trump—the obnoxious boss who has become the benchmark hero. Managers need to listen, show patience, coach individuals and teams, invest in more than one strategy toward solutions, and convey a willingness to change trajectory.

Robert Driscoll, a retired hospital administrator, insisted that a good leader can use dissent as a valuable tool:

> It can be the catalyst for change, improvement, and may even turn the dissenting individual into a lead member of a team. The assumption here is that the organization has high ethical standards that are recognized by staff and that such standards are applied without exception. I have often found that productivity is enhanced when there is dissent at an open or department meeting. Rather than being defensive, a good manager may acknowledge diverse opinions and engage the group.

Finally, these leaders emphasized that once a decision is made, managers need to complete the loop and communicate the reasons for the decision. Acknowledge consideration of other options that were suggested and explain why they were not chosen.

Listen

More than half of the managers who responded to my survey cited listening as one of the most important ways to manage dissent. This means listening not only to the actual words being said but also to what is behind the language of dissent. This involves communicating that one is looking for the best solution, then tuning into the underlying reasons for, or root problems of, the dissent. As Karl Sleight, former director of the New York State Ethics Commission, put it:

> The hallmark of a strong leader is to be a good listener. Not just hear the dissent, but to probe it, evaluate it, challenge the underpinnings (without discarding it out of hand), and make a reasoned decision on whether the dissent has a viable position. The value of simply paying attention to dissent should not be underestimated. If the members of the organization know that the leader is

comfortable with his/her leadership position, so to allow (even embrace) differing points of view, dissent can breed loyalty and a stronger organization. Obviously, the converse is also very true.

Peter Boice, a Department of Defense conservation team leader, suggested that managers slowly build up trust by listening, but do it as early as possible. "Ask those lower in the chain to contribute to policy development," offered Boice. "Actually demonstrate that you're willing to listen by making changes based on input. . . . Seek input before it boils up to dissent, but is viewed rather as productive objections. I really think that it is key to act before one gets to the point of dissent; at that point the stakes are higher, the battle lines drawn."

Lisa Blomgren Bingham, former director of the Indiana Conflict Resolution Institute and one of the evaluators of the U.S. Postal Service REDRESS dispute system, emphasized that managers need to learn to *just listen*. The REDRESS program was initiated in response to people "going postal"—increased incidents of violence, aggression, anger, and conflict in the postal service. Researchers found that postal service managers, when approached by a dissenting employee, felt it was their duty to stick up for the organization and rebut, point by point, every negative statement made by the accuser. Dispute resolution experts taught the managers to *just listen*. This, coupled with a proactive mediation program, yielded a documented drop in aggression, conflict, and complaints at the U.S. Postal Service.

The generalizable lesson here for managers is not to act defensively when approached by a potential guerrilla, and to not feel the need to immediately cite chapter and verse of the applicable regulation in defense of the organization. Instead, they need to *listen*. Not only will this open up channels of communication, but also by simply listening a manager can learn valuable information that may in fact improve the workings of the organization and at the very least will give the manager a better sense of the guerrilla's perspective. Managers also need the authority to settle insubordinate disputes at their infancy in order to process and resolve early the conflicts that impel guerrilla activity.

Marty Hanson, head of the Department of Access and Preservation at a large university research library offered:

> A leader can make dissent productive by *listening* to the voices of dissent, finding out what is at the root of their dissent, looking for and listening to people in the organization who are angry (the loyal opposition), for an angry voice insinuates that an individual still cares about the organization. Productive dissent forestalls "coercive harmony" (a term coined by anthropologist Laura Nader), when the abnormal becomes normal, when "harmony coerced is freedom lost."

One manager wrote that a leader in an organization "needs to be a listener and not one whose fixation on the ultimate organizational goal makes him or her lose sight of common sense, humanity, or common norms." Another anonymous manager, a hospital administrator, gave these concrete tips: "When a member is dissenting, ask, 'How could your view make a better outcome?'—as contrasted to, 'I don't agree.' Encourage everyone to offer opinions by going all around the group and asking for individual input from each and every individual."

Others who recommended listening in an open, honest fashion also cautioned managers not to "take it personally." Know that some form of dissent is a normal organizational dynamic. Appreciate the challenge as an opportunity to grow, an opportunity to build a team, and an opportunity to gather data in order to make the best decision possible. "By accepting dissent as a product of the organization's current culture and not interpreting it as a personal indictment, a leader can intellectually process the causes of the dissent without becoming emotionally sidetracked," emphasized Brian Lock, assistant director of the Washington Commission for National and Community Service.

Earl Meredith, a manager at the National Oceanic and Atmospheric Administration, summed up his advice concerning managing dissent as follows: "Listen to it. Consider it. Understand it. Translate it for others so all can understand it. Be respectful while debating and reformulate it into a more easily acceptable presentation to the organization if it turns out to be beneficial, yet still unpalatable to the organization."

My respondents' advice to listen is supported by the empirical research. Researchers who examined rule adherence among law enforcement officers and soldiers found that procedural justice, including being listened to, within an organization is central to rule adherence (Tyler, Callahan, and Frost 2007).

Understand the Formal and Informal Organization

The majority of managers who responded to my survey emphasized that leaders must understand the organization both formally and informally. The informal organization, generally, is that which may not manifest itself on an organization chart or in official documents. Examples include histories and connections between and among employees, traditions, power bases, and how the organization has learned to cope with challenges. Cooper (2012) explains the importance of this concept for ethical decision making:

> Complying with the organization's informal norms and procedures is ordinarily required of a responsible public administrator. These are the specific organizational means for structuring and maintaining work that is consistent with the organization's legitimate mission. Because not everything can be written down formally, and recognizing that informally evolved norms give cohesion and identity to an organization, these unofficial patterns of practice play an essential role.
>
> However, at times these controls may subvert the mission or detract from its achievement, as in goal displacement. A truly responsible administrator will bear an obligation to propose changes when they become problematic for the

wishes of the public, inconsistent with professional judgment, or in conflict with personal conscience. It is irresponsible to simply ignore or circumvent inappropriate norms and procedures on the one hand, or reluctantly comply with them on the other. (256–257)

The informal organization may be more difficult to identify, but it is often the environment within which dissent grows and develops. Dissent coming from the informal organization may be solely a sign of some disgruntled employees, or it may be a legitimate, telltale sign of a significant issue within the organization. Dissent becomes productive when the members of the organization recognize and believe that the leaders are honestly concerned about them and are willing to work on making positive changes. At the same time, dissenters must also recognize that the structure of some organizations (such as military and paramilitary organizations) will prevent certain types of changes.

A former staff person of a large international nonprofit environmental group advised:

> Listen to the informal organization. Listen to the members/followers/staff and let them know that they are heard. In addition, ask a trusted staff person to have their ear to the ground of the informal organization to give you feedback. Prevent needless arguments right away with communication, and make sure there is clear communication about what the dissent is over, especially if it is about current organizational policy. In my experience the members/followers/staff didn't understand the policy, and once they did their demands were pretty much reduced to nothing. It was all misunderstanding. But the whole incident highlighted formal and informal flaws in the organizational structure and allowed us to implement better communication strategies.

Separate the People from the Problem

More than half of those who responded to my survey emphasized the need to approach the issues on the merits and people as human beings. Fisher and Ury reinforce this in their best-selling book *Getting to Yes* (2011), where they advise separating the relationship from the substance, dealing directly with the people problem, and striving to solve the problem at hand collaboratively.

Sharon Halinan, a contracting officer at the EPA, put it this way:

> Leaders must listen beyond the words and tone of the dissenters, as sometimes their message is simply delivered the wrong way, and the message itself is valid. Leaders must try to understand where the dissenters are coming from; this shows respect for people, and that can go a long way. When leaders handle dissent with respect, professional courtesy, and, when necessary, the decision to "agree to disagree," people at least know they have been heard, which sends powerful messages that the employees can speak out and will be heard.

Vito Sciscioli, director of operations for the city of Syracuse, New York, commented:

> The most important thing regarding managing dissent is to make sure the dissenting opinion is what is addressed and not the person delivering it. Also, creating an atmosphere of "I mean you no harm" is critical to establishing an environment where the free flow of ideas is possible.

Create Multiple Channels for Dissent

Many of the more seasoned leaders who responded to my survey emphasized that it is important to realize that dissent happens in every organization. Therefore, if leaders and managers create a process that allows for dissent, employees will feel they can express their views, and disagreements will be channeled into something productive. If dissent is stifled, it will only cause resentment. Set up a regular process to receive dissent. Be accessible. Have an open-door policy. Insist that employees come to you first. Make evaluation a two-way street, with managers evaluating those they supervise and employees evaluating their supervisors. Allow employees to dissent in civil discourse in group meetings or in private through memos or conversations; some people who have great ideas that challenge the status quo do not like to display their ideas publicly.

The director of the Office of Resource Management for the U.S. Department of Energy advised: "Set up a regular process to receive dissent. Lay the ground rules for civil discourse. Actively listen to it. Act upon it and follow up to ensure that there was action."

The chief of corrections for the state of Tennessee wrote:

> Listen to your people. They are the number one asset of an organization. Do this by getting out and about. Talking with employees individually and in groups. Know their jobs, frustrations, and things that motivate them. Obviously every idea or complaint cannot be acted on or resolved, but many people feel better once they have had an opportunity to "talk to the boss." A manager must take steps to act on the issues in a timely manner. Sometimes sitting two employees or groups of employees down who appear to have conflict can be positive. When facilitated, the employees can air out their differences, learn a little about each other and their jobs, and create a more positive work environment.

Mitchel Audritsch, a business manager, emphasized:

> Never shoot messengers. Good findings come from dissent. Penalizing the messenger on the basis of the message will encourage dissent going underground—where the organization won't benefit and the dissent metastasizes into destructive dissent. Don't penalize risk taking. Dissent manifests itself in taking risks. Holding people up to 100 percent success thresholds will encourage timidity. . . . Ask for critical appraisals of work, style, approach, direction. A

clear and consistent message from leadership about wanting open critical thinking about every aspect of the leader's role is essential. Guarantee the anonymity of critics. The universal assumption is that critics are sought for the sole purpose of disciplining them. Leaders must accept this as a natural condition. Therefore, any mechanism for soliciting the honest dissent of staff must absolutely guarantee anonymity.

Create Dissent Boundaries and Know When to Stop

"Dissent is important," former NASA head Sean O'Keefe told me, "but a leader has to know when to say 'enough.' If taken too far, dissent can be like pulling the thread of a sweater too long and hard . . . eventually the sweater unravels." To illustrate this point O'Keefe talked about his order to his staff and his promise to Congress after the *Columbia* space shuttle disaster. He ordered the implementation of every one of the fifteen items labeled by the *Columbia* Accident Investigation Board (CAIB) as necessary before another space shuttle was launched. Dozens of discussions took place among staff members about their being forced to comply with all fifteen points, and there were plenty of dissenters. Some wanted to implement a few items, but not all. Many argued about the wisdom of the CAIB recommendations themselves. But in the end O'Keefe determined that in order to assure a safer space shuttle program, he had to order that all fifteen items be implemented. End of discussion.

Both O'Keefe and Dan Crippen, former director of the Congressional Budget Office (CBO), emphasized how helpful peer review was to them in bringing dissent between and among professionals in their organizations to a close. O'Keefe used formal groups, like the National Science Foundation and the statutorily mandated NASA Aerospace Safety Advisory Committee, as well as informal groups such as the Return to Flight Task Group (assembled as required under the Federal Advisory Committee Act) to render expert opinions. Crippen hired Karen Lewis, Sondheimer Professor of International Economics and Finance at the Wharton School of the University of Pennsylvania, to help him sort out the diversity of analyses and opinions he was receiving from CBO staff. Crippen also had many CBO analyses and publications sent to experts outside the organization for examination before they were widely disseminated.

Moss Cail, development manager at the Arts and Business Council of Chicago, suggested:

> Accept dissent as a productive and positive part of the decision making process. From the start the manager should make two things clear: (1) I am willing to hear all thoughts on a matter either publicly or privately; (2) do not, under any circumstances, voice dissent publicly without first speaking with me about your concerns. I believe that this up-front, honest dialogue helps to keep all the positive aspects of dissent, while keeping many of the negative aspects under as much control as is possible.

An anonymous manager put it another way:

While managers need to create avenues for dissent, they also need to create boundaries that limit how dissent is offered—so as to keep the focus on the reason for the dissent and the action. If these boundaries are not created, the discussion quickly changes to one of process and not substance when someone dissents in a manner that might be considered improper. Another way to keep dissent productive is to require managers to seek dissent. For example, if a report requires agreement between an entire team or across teams, requiring the manager to seek formal approval across the board before moving forward might ensure that various perspectives are heard.

Kurt Fenstermacher, director of the Office of Solid Waste Management in Lehigh County, Pennsylvania, wrote: "Harness the dissenters . . . listen to the dissent issue, analyze the current situation, assess how the dissent would change current operations/issues. Allowing the dissent to continue without genuine acknowledgment will escalate the dissension." This means leading by setting the stage, creating rules for dissenters, and enforcing them. Also, managers should encourage dissenting individuals to provide more background and research to back up their opinions.

Steve Sarcozy, city manager of Bellevue, Washington, recommended that managers

lead by "principals" established well in advance of a decision point. Request coworkers/managers/staff to brainstorm or create a vision in the area of question (a range of options from which the manager/decision maker can select, presumably with a broad set of objectives). Insist that any dissent is quickly responded to, resolved, and proceed with the outcome—without further discussion (with prejudice) of any type.

Keith Parks, sheriff's commander in Ventura, California, opined:

In all that a leader does, a positive and respectful environment must be maintained. Allowing dissent to occur, within the boundaries set by respect and civility toward the opinions and backgrounds of others within the organization, can bring ideas to the forefront for consideration.

Dan Fiorino, formerly of the EPA, added:

A leader can be open to differing views and give people an outlet to express their opinions. An open atmosphere where dissent is possible if done right is good for an organization. At the same time, a leader should not let people take advantage of the situation by using dissent as a distraction from personal or performance problems. Tolerance for different views should be balanced with holding people accountable for their actions and making decisions on issues, no matter what the dissenters say.

Finally, Susan Livingstone, former undersecretary of the U.S. Navy, added this to the discussion:

> Encourage dissent, value dissent, have the ego to deal with dissent, but don't make dissent a nonproductive value. A leader who seeks dissent and welcomes alternative opinions is good. But a leader who values those more than the message being conveyed sends the wrong message . . . both in terms of his/her leadership capabilities to discern the truth and his/her ability to sort through the complexities. A leader needs to seek, sort, and decide. The decisions made will convey to others how productive dissent is.

CONCLUSION

I spent a Sunday at NASA headquarters in Washington, D.C., working with a group that was finalizing the report of the Return to Flight Task Group. We spent the morning perfecting the executive summary and then broke for lunch. At lunch I sat across from Dan Crippen. "I'm working on a book on managing dissent in public organizations. How did you manage dissent while director of the Congressional Budget Office?" I asked Crippen. "You'll see this afternoon," Crippen said, with a strange look on his face.

That afternoon I found myself in a meeting with Crippen and six NASA staff members. Half the staff were career civil servants, and the other half were contract employees. Crippen asked the executive secretary of the RTF TG to leave the room. The executive secretary left and never came back that day. The professional editor of our report explained that the two former astronauts who chaired the RTF TG were insisting that only positive insights, analyses, and observations about NASA be included in the task group's final report. It wasn't a question of telling mistruths, but a question of not telling the whole story. A group of RTF TG members and NASA staff, led by Crippen, felt a need to tell the whole story "because it is the right thing to do." Crippen and others repeatedly asked the task group chairs to include dissenting opinions in the final report. They were repeatedly rebuffed. The plan was to write a dissenting report, publish it, and launch it on the NASA website, against the wishes of the RTF TG cochairs. Was I with them or against them?

What ensued was a two-hour meeting devoted to plotting how to publish a supplemental dissenting report. I went around the room and asked pointed questions:

O'Leary: How can you get such a report published without the cochairs' signature?

Editor: I don't need their signature. The NASA printer will publish anything I bring them and we still have money in the budget.

O'Leary: Why do you want to do this?

Editor: Because it is the right thing to do. The American public deserves to know the whole truth. When I was an editor of the CAIB report, Admiral Gehman allowed any and all dissent to be voiced and printed. He asked for people to challenge him. He insisted on a diversity of views. He probed for the hard questions. I learned from him the right way to manage dissent.

O'Leary: You could get in trouble.

Editor: This is the right thing to do. I don't care if I get in trouble. What can they do to me once it's printed—yell at me? Besides, I'm a contract employee and I won't be around NASA for long.

O'Leary: What about the other five staff members?

At this point Crippen joined the conversation.

Crippen: We'll protect the "gold badges," the civil servants. The contract employees are moving on to other assignments in ten days. I'll even go to bat for the gold badges inside NASA if needed. This is the right thing to do. The public deserves the truth. I have repeatedly voiced my objections publicly and privately to our cochairs. I have met with the new NASA administrator and several other top NASA officials, telling them that this is coming. Each has responded that they'd rather have the truth come out than suppress dissent. We don't want another *Columbia* or *Challenger* disaster.

O'Leary [to the   Why are you doing this?
other staff]:

The staff then took turns telling stories about the need to bring to light problems with NASA's management and NASA's seeming inability to learn from past mistakes. "NASA is in denial," one staff member said. "The agency needs to be confronted with the truth."

In stumbled the chief public relations officer of the RTF TG, who was briefed on the purpose of our meeting. He obviously was surprised, but he then ended up coaching the group on the challenges of such an approach, how to avoid the appearance of "sour grapes," and different avenues we could pursue. "This is an art, not a science," he said. "Are you sure you've exhausted all other appropriate channels? Try again to have these viewpoints allowed in the final report, then if rejected follow through with your plan. But I know nothing about this meeting. Be sure to get the dissent on the record at the public meeting tomorrow so it doesn't look like sour grapes after the fact. Did I mention that I know nothing about this meeting?"

He refused to launch the dissenting report on the website without appropriate permission, but this did not deter the group. He emphasized that while he could not help us formally, he would help us informally. He closed by saying again that if anyone asked, he knew nothing about our meeting.

The group then outlined what would go into the dissenting report, divided up responsibilities, and exchanged personal e-mail addresses. No e-mails among us were to be sent on or to NASA accounts. I looked at Crippen. "This is what my book is about," I said. "I know," he responded with a grin. "Remember what I said to you at lunch today?"

Like the two former astronauts who headed up the RTF TG, leaders can easily become imprisoned in, and blinded by, their own thoughts and feelings about dissent because they are locked into their own "worlds." They may be concerned solely with the particulars of their own careers, their own programs, or their own experiences. In the day-to-day grind of public service, managers' overwhelming preoccupation with what comes across their desks may lead them to ignore another more fundamental level of reality. When managers fail to see the whole picture, when they neglect the perspective of open systems, of wholeness and connectedness, and of open communications, they see only one side of the dissent issue: it is a "problem," dissenters are a "pain," "a thorn in my side," "an annoyance to deal with."

While this may be true, it is also true that there is another, very real dimension that goes beyond individual managers' own experiences. When managers identify only with a permanent, impermeable view of their organizations and what ideas are appropriate for those organizations, that is a form of blindness. It takes true work to break out of the prison of such narrow thoughts.

We all want our public organizations to be open to new ideas, yet many good ideas go undeveloped in these organizations because they deviate from the normal ways of doing things. Our public programs need to be pushed out of their safety zones—those places of mental and physical routine and normalcy—so that those who run them can start to think differently. Organizational denial, when present, needs to be confronted.

As a political appointee public manager in the 1980s, I used to laugh whenever someone advocated turning our agency into a "learning organization" because there was simply no time to stop running, no time to pause, no time to think, and no time to reflect. I was working seventy-hour weeks, which I likened to playing tennis at the net day in and day out. There was no time to take the long view, to play tennis at the baseline, and certainly no time to get off the court and think about the action. Public employees need enough time to understand the totality of the issues they are addressing. In our highly pressurized work environments, with their pushes and pulls from many constituencies and multiple directions, this can be difficult.

Leaders should encourage divergent thinking, not quash it. An organization culture that welcomes what Sean O'Keefe calls "diversity thinking" is essential. Sociologists have concluded that new ideas often come from managers' contacts outside their immediate work groups (Erard 2004; Burt 2004). Hence the building of networks, both formal and informal, should be encouraged when appropriate.

Early, cautious evidence derived from studies of networks indicates that "working through network structures provides a way of dealing with 'wicked problems' by bringing about systemic change. In the process, innovation and change in traditional methods of operation come to the fore" (Keast, Mandell, Brown, and Woolcock 2004, 370). The networks manifested in the episodes in this book offered "reality checks" for ideas that had been incubating in the far recesses of government offices. The networks also allowed ideas to cross-pollinate. Last, the networks helped employees break out of status quo thinking.

Finally, government leaders need to invest in whole organization dispute systems. The challenges of guerrilla government will never cease to exist. Like the returning waves of the ocean, they will ebb and flow. The waves may be changed, lessened, or softened by dispute management systems, but they will remain a fact of life for all public managers. Having multiple internal organizational outlets for potential and actual guerrillas and their ideas will only strengthen our public agencies. The survival and vibrancy of our public organizations depend on it.

As it turned out, when the NASA RTF TG had its last meeting, the day after the secret meeting with Crippen and the staff, several outraged members publicly voiced loud opposition to the idea of a "sanitized," "whitewashed" report. The dissenting views spilled over into the public meeting, and the two cochairs were forced to retreat from their insistence on a purely positive report. Yet, because only part of the information that had concerned the dissenters was allowed in the final report, Crippen and the rest of us were still secretly debating whether we would write and publish a smaller dissenting report on the items that remained. Whether we did so is for me to know and for you to find out.

NOTE

1. Survey respondents were given the option of self-identifying or remaining anonymous. In some instances respondents identified themselves to me but asked that I not reveal their identities. Hence some quotes are attributed to specific individuals while others are not.

Postlude: Are There Lessons?

MANY PEOPLE wonder why it took me years to write this slim book. Half of the answer lies with the difficulty in interviewing government guerrillas, who generally do not want to be interviewed. The other half lies with the ethical and moral questions posed by guerrilla government, which are not easy to answer. Here are some of the most compelling questions that have arisen in my years of studying and discussing guerrilla government. I offer them here to challenge us all to insist on diversity of thought and to better manage dissent in our public organizations.

IN GENERAL

1. Do you agree or disagree, generally, with the actions of the guerrillas profiled in this book?
2. Of the many episodes of guerrilla government woven throughout this book, are there specific stories that resonate with you? Are there stories that repel you? Why?
3. Does subject area make a difference? If the guerrillas profiled in this book had been white supremacist zealots, would that change your analysis of their actions?
4. What is the "dark side" of guerrilla government? Can you offer examples from the popular press?
5. Reread Box 6.1, "Guidelines for Guerrillas from Guerrillas." Which, if any, of the listed guidelines do you accept as legitimate? Which do you reject? Again, does context matter?
6. Does transparency matter? Are certain actions by government guerrillas more acceptable if we know about them? If yes, which ones? If no, why not?
7. Read the following excerpt from a recent journal article by public administration scholar Larry Lynn (2012). Examine Lynn's ideas with this question in mind: What if the system is wrong?

Public administrators must not pursue a public interest they alone define. The public interest is defined by the public and, in our system of government, that means the institutions established pursuant to constitutional principles of delegation and accountability. In public service, no element of administrative integrity is more important.

8. If you are a government guerrilla, how do you *really* know when or if you are right? Where do you draw the line between sincere concern and arrogant hubris?
9. When do the ends justify the means?
10. At what point is professionalism violated by guerrilla government?
11. In addition to the suggestions in this book, what are some concrete, proactive steps that managers can take to stem the occurrence of guerrilla government?
12. I recently received the following e-mail messages from two of my former students. What do you think of their perspectives?

Dear Professor O'Leary,

I work in a local government in the state of Washington. As far as I can think, I've not clandestinely acted disobediently because it was the right thing to do. I don't think clandestine actions are the right thing to do when an ethical issue is on the line. Rather, forthright and open disobedience is the right thing to do. Those who are requesting unethical actions deserve to know that you feel they've crossed an ethical line. Otherwise, how can behavior be improved and/or issues be vetted? So far, when I've put my foot down on an issue, my superiors have either backed down or found someone else to do the work.

Dear Professor O'Leary,

Your work on guerrilla government really upsets me. A public servant has a duty to obey all orders given by superiors. If one disagrees with those orders, the proper thing to do is to quit and find another job. Guerrilla government activity is always wrong.

CHAPTER 2: GUERRILLA GOVERNMENT AND THE NEVADA WETLANDS

1. Do you think the Nevada Four could have been as entrepreneurial as they were (e.g., in fund-raising) had they worked solely within their own bureaucracies?
2. When, if ever, is it appropriate to use government funds for your own cause?
3. What do you think of the Nevada Four's handling of the fish kill incident? Was this ethical behavior for a scientist? For a public servant?
4. Was it ethical for the Nevada Four to invite the U.S. senator to tour the refuge but tell their superiors that the senator requested the tour?
5. One of the Nevada Four who later became a refuge manager says that he gives chapter 2 of this book to all his new employees and tells them, "This is the way we do business here." What do you think of that?

6. Another of the Nevada Four who later transferred voluntarily to another DOI site used the "techniques" described in chapter 2 in his new setting, and subsequently reported, "I've fallen on my sword." When he was caught carrying out guerrilla government activities, he was cut out of all major decision-making meetings, moved to a windowless office, and told to mind his own business. What do you think of that?

CHAPTER 3: GUERRILLA GOVERNMENT IN THE EPA'S SEATTLE REGIONAL OFFICE

1. Were the actions of the Seattle EPA staff justified? Why or why not?
2. If you think of the Reagan administration political appointees as the guerrillas, does this change your analysis of the case?
3. Were the Seattle EPA staff members the embodiment of stubborn and misguided institutionalization—long-timers who represented a culture different from that of the new political leaders voted in by the American people?
4. Is there a difference ethically between a concerned public servant seeking out the support of an elected official and a concerned public servant seeking out the support of the media?
5. Contrast the management style of Ernesta Barnes to that of John Spencer and Robie Russell. Are there lessons to be gleaned from such a comparison?
6. Should career public servants "just suck it up" (to quote one of my graduate students) and loyally follow new political appointees even when they feel there is a lack of objective decision making?
7. What were the other options available to the Seattle EPA staff?

CHAPTER 4: A GOVERNMENT GUERRILLA SUES HIS OWN AGENCY

1. Under the Multiple Use–Sustained Yield Act of 1960, the Forest Service is explicitly granted the authority to manage the national forests for recreation, grazing, wildlife, fisheries, and wilderness, in addition to timber and watershed purposes. How does this factor into the Claude Ferguson story?
2. Put yourself in Ferguson's shoes. How do you know you are right?
3. Does Ferguson's admitted love of hunting raise a question of conflict of interest concerning his stance on ORV use in the national forest?
4. Could Ferguson have been captive to local interests as Kaufman describes in *The Forest Ranger*? Why or why not?
5. Reread Box 4.1, "Claude Ferguson's Clashing Obligations." How might a public servant make sense of the paradox these obligations raise?
6. Those who wrote letters against Ferguson's actions (Box 4.3) largely felt that he should not be blasting the Forest Service ORV policy in public. Should career public servants be able to criticize their own bureaucracies publicly? First,

make the case that they should not be allowed to do so, then present all the reasons they should be able to do so.

7. Don Girton (Ferguson's boss) said, "If you must condemn and you must criticize externally, I think it gets to the point where the individual had better just resign his position and pursue his course of action—if he feels that strongly about it." Do you agree or disagree with this statement?

8. Later Girton said that Ferguson had always been against the idea of ORV use in the forest and that he "disguised" his beliefs so he could attack the policy. Put yourself in Girton's shoes. How would you know whether this was true or not?

CHAPTER 5: WIKILEAKS AND GUERRILLA GOVERNMENT

1. Is the case of Private First Class Bradley Manning different from the other cases presented in this book? Why or why not?

2. Did Manning act ethically or unethically? Explain.

3. Was it ethical for Manning to make public diplomatic cables with the names of informants?

4. Was it right for PayPal, banks, and credit card companies to refuse to do business with WikiLeaks and not process payments to the organization?

5. Should newspapers such as the *New York Times* and the *Guardian* of London have published portions of the leaked cables as they did?

6. One analysis of the Manning-WikiLeaks case says, "If the weight of public need for this information overwhelmed the public need for security then . . . [Manning] did the right thing" (Lennon 2010, 9). What do you think of this statement?

7. How would you answer the questions posed in this *New York Times* blog post?

   Secretary of State Hillary Rodham Clinton argued that disclosures of classified information "tear at the fabric" of government, "sabotaging peaceful relations between nations." What arguments can be made to support and rebut Mrs. Clinton's perspective? Can leaks like this threaten the proper function of government and the maintenance of peace between nations? (Kavanagh and Ojalvo 2010)

8. Could the WikiLeaks scandal have been prevented? Should it have been prevented?

9. Are there any lessons to be learned from the Manning-WikiLeaks case that can be generalized to the everyday workplace?

10. Millenials have grown up with the internet, Facebook, Twitter, and other forms of social media, in an era of share-anything-with-everyone that's clearly different from previous generations. Will this "Let me tell my friends where I am and post amazing photos of me doing amazing things" philosophy, as well as a "Let's see if we can make this go viral" daring, increase the incidents of guerrilla government around the world?

References

Aberbach, J. D., and B. A. Rockman. 2000. *In the Web of Politics: Three Decades of the U.S. Federal Executive*. Washington, DC: Brookings Institution Press.

———. 2006. "The Past and Future of Political-Administrative Relations: Research from *Bureaucrats and Politicians* to *In the Web of Politics*—and Beyond." *International Journal of Public Administration* 29 (12): 977–995.

Adams, G. B., and D. L. Balfour. 2009. *Unmasking Administrative Evil*. 3rd ed. Armonk, NY: M. E. Sharpe.

Agranoff, R., and M. McGuire. 2004. *Collaborative Public Management: New Strategies for Local Governments*. Washington, DC: Georgetown University Press.

Aldrich, H. F. 1972. "An Organization-Environment Perspective on Cooperation and Conflict between Organizations and the Manpower Training System." In *Conflict and Power in Complex Organizations: An Inter-institutional Perspective,* ed. A. R. Negandhi. Kent, OH: Comparative Administrative Research Institute.

Alford, C. F. 2002. *Whistleblowers: Broken Lives and Organizational Power*. Ithaca, NY: Cornell University Press.

———. 2007. "Whistleblower Narratives: The Experience of the Choiceless Choice." *Social Research* 74 (1): 223–248.

Allison, G., and P. Zelikow 1999. *Essence of Decision: Explaining the Cuban Missile Crisis*. 2nd ed. New York: Little, Brown.

Anglin, R. 1989. "You Don't Own the Blood of Mother Earth." U.S. Department of the Interior. Paper presented to the National Academy of Sciences/National Research Council, Committee on Western Water Management, Reno, NV, October 26.

Appleby, P. 1949. *Policy and Administration*. Birmingham: University of Alabama Press.

Bandura, A. 1978. *Social Learning Theory*. Englewood Cliffs, NJ: Prentice-Hall.

Barringer, F. 1983. "EPA Asks Residents' Advice about Arsenic Plant." *Washington Post,* July 14.

Baumgartner, F. R., and B. D. Jones. 2009. *Agendas and Instability in American Politics*. 2nd ed. Chicago: University of Chicago Press.

Bendor, J., S. Taylor, and R. Van Gaalen. 1985. "Bureaucratic Expertise versus Legislative Authority: A Model of Deception and Monitoring in Budgeting." *American Political Science Review* 79 (4): 1041–1060.

Benveniste, G. 1977. *The Politics of Expertise.* 2nd ed. Berkeley, CA: Boyd and Fraser.

Bernstein, C., and B. Woodward. 1974. *All the President's Men.* New York: Simon & Schuster.

Bingham, L., and R. O'Leary, eds. 2008. *Big Ideas in Collaborative Public Management.* Armonk, NY: M. E. Sharpe.

Blau, J. R. 1979. "Expertise and Power in Professional Organizations." *Sociology of Work and Occupations* 6 (1): 103–123.

Bouville, M. 2008. "Whistle-Blowing and Morality." *Journal of Business Ethics* 81 (3): 579–585.

Brehm, J., and S. Gates. 1997. *Working, Shirking, and Sabotage: Bureaucratic Response to a Democratic Public.* Ann Arbor: University of Michigan Press.

Brewer, G. A., S. C. Selden, and Rex L. Facer II. 2000. "Individual Conceptions of Public Service Motivation." *Public Administration Review* 60 (3): 254–264.

Brock, J. 1998. "The Politics of Establishing Urban Growth Areas in St. Claire County." Electronic Hallway at the Evans School of Public Affairs, University of Washington, Seattle.

Brouwer, S., and F. Biermann. 2011. "Towards Adaptive Management: Examining the Strategies of Policy Entrepreneurs in Dutch Water Management." *Ecology and Society* 16 (4), art. 5.

Brower, R. S., and M. Y. Abolafia. 1997. "Bureaucratic Politics: The View from Below." *Journal of Public Administration Research and Theory* 7 (2): 305–331.

Brownlow, L. 1959. *A Passion for Anonymity.* Chicago: University of Chicago Press.

Bruhn, J. G. 2009. "The Functionality of Gray Area Ethics in Organizations." *Journal of Business Ethics* 89 (2): 205–214.

Bumiller, E. 2010. "Army Broadens Inquiry into WikiLeaks Disclosure." *New York Times,* July 30.

Burns, J. F., and R. Somaiya. 2010. "WikiLeaks Founder Gets Support in Rebuking U.S. on Whistle-Blowers." *New York Times,* October 23.

Burt, R. S. 2004. "Structural Holes and Good Ideas." *American Journal of Sociology* 110 (2): 349–399.

Caldwell, C., and M. Canuto-Carranco. 2010. "'Organizational Terrorism' and Moral Choices: Exercising Voice When the Leader Is the Problem." *Journal of Business Ethics* 97 (1): 159–171.

Carpenter, S. L., and W. J. D. Kennedy. 2001. *Managing Public Disputes: A Practical Guide for Government, Business, and Citizens' Groups.* 2nd ed. San Francisco: Jossey-Bass.

Cleveland, H. 1956. "Executives in the Political Jungle." *Annals of the American Association of Political Science* 307 (September): 37–47.

Clines, F. X., and B. Weinraub. 1981. "Briefing." *New York Times,* November 10.

Cook, B. J. 1996. *Bureaucracy and Self-Government: Reconsidering the Role of Public Administration in American Politics.* Baltimore: Johns Hopkins University Press.

Cooper, T. L., ed. 2001. *Handbook of Administrative Ethics,* 2nd ed. New York: Marcel Dekker.

———. 2012. *The Responsible Administrator: An Approach to Ethics for the Administrative Role.* 6th ed. San Francisco: Jossey-Bass.

Costantino, C. A., and C. S. Merchant. 1996. *Designing Conflict Management Systems: A Guide to Creating Productive and Healthy Organizations.* San Francisco: Jossey-Bass.

Couto, R. A. 1991. "Heroic Bureaucracies." *Administration and Society* 23 (1): 123–147.

Cronin, T. E. 1980. *The State of the Presidency.* 2nd ed. New York: Little, Brown.

Cyert, R. M., and J. G. March. 1992. *A Behavioral Theory of the Firm.* 2nd ed. Englewood Cliffs, NJ: Prentice-Hall.

Davis, S. 1987a. "Wildlife Disaster." KGO-TV (San Francisco) *Evening News* multinight special, March 23–27.

———. 1987b. "Death of a Refuge." KGO-TV (San Francisco) *Evening News* multinight special, April 20–24.

De Graaf, G. 2010. "A Report on Reporting: Why Peers Report Integrity and Law Violations in Public Organizations." *Public Administration Review* 70 (5): 767–779.

DeHart-Davis, L. 2007. "The Unbureaucratic Personality." *Public Administration Review* 67 (5): 892–903.

De Maria, W. 2008. "Whistleblowers and Organizational Protesters: Crossing Imaginary Borders." *Current Sociology* 56 (6): 865–883.

Denhardt, K. 1988. *The Ethics of Public Service: Resolving Moral Dilemmas in Public Organizations.* New York: Greenwood Press.

Dietrich, B. 1990a. "Regional EPA Chief Quits, May Run for Office in Idaho." *Seattle Times,* January 29.

———. 1990b. "Regional EPA Chief Blocked Cleanup in Idaho, Says Audit." *Seattle Times,* February 27.

Dobel, J. P. 1999. *Public Integrity.* Baltimore: Johns Hopkins University Press.

Doig, J. W., and E. C. Hargrove, eds. 1987. *Leadership and Innovation: A Biographical Perspective on Entrepreneurs in Government.* Baltimore: Johns Hopkins University Press.

Dolan, J. 1987. "Dateline: Washington." UPI, July 21. http://www.upi.com.

Downs, A. 1993. *Inside Bureaucracy.* New York: Waveland Press. (Original work published 1967)

Dunn, D. R. 1970. "Motorized Recreation Vehicles . . . On Borrowed Time." *Parks and Recreation,* July.

Ellis, L. 1977. "Off-Road Vehicles Facing Ban in Hoosier Forest?" *Louisville Courier-Journal,* October 19.

Emery, F. E., and E. L. Trist. 1965. "The Causal Texture of Organizational Environments." *Human Relations* 18: 21–32.

Erard, M. 2004. "Where to Get a Good Idea: Steal It Outside Your Group." *New York Times,* May 22.

Ermann, M. D., and R. J. Lundman. 1978. "Deviant Acts by Complex Organizations: Deviance and Social Control at the Organizational Level of Analysis." *Sociological Quarterly* 19 (1): 55–67.

Farrell, D. 1983. "Exit, Voice, Loyalty, and Neglect as Responses to Job Dissatisfaction: A Multidimensional Scaling Study." *Academy of Management Journal* 26 (4): 596–607.

Feldman, M. S. 1989. *Order without Design: Information Production and Policy Making.* Stanford, CA: Stanford University Press.

Fisher, R., and W. Ury, with B. Patton, ed. 2011. *Getting to Yes: Negotiating Agreement without Giving In.* 3rd ed. New York: Penguin.

Fitzgerald, A. E. 1989. *The Pentagonists: An Insider's View of Waste, Mismanagement, and Fraud in Defense Spending.* Boston: Houghton Mifflin.

Flash, C. 1987. "Regional Hazardous Waste Conference Planned." UPI, March 11. http://www.upi.com.

Fleishman, J. L. 1981. "Self-Interest and Political Integrity." In *Public Duties: The Moral Obligations of Government Officials,* ed. J. L. Fleishman and M. H. Moore. Cambridge, MA: Harvard University Press.

Frederickson, H. G. 1991. "Toward a Theory of the Public for Public Administration." *Administration and Society* 22 (4): 395–417.

Frey, J. H. 1982. "Controlling Deviant Organizations: Scientists as Moral Entrepreneurs." *California Sociologist* 5 (1): 33–50.

Gailmard, S., and J. W. Patty. 2007. "Slackers and Zealots: Civil Service, Policy Discretion, and Bureaucratic Expertise." *American Journal of Political Science* 51 (4): 873–889.

Gaus, J. 1947. *Reflections on Public Administration.* Birmingham: University of Alabama Press.

Gawthrop, L. C. 1998. *Public Service and Democracy: Ethical Imperatives for the 21st Century.* New York: Chatham House.

Getha-Taylor, H. 2009. "Where's (Dwight) Waldo?" *Public Performance and Management Review* 32 (4): 574–578.

Gilbreath, M. 1986. "New EPA Regional Chief Seeks Improved Communication." UPI, August 11. http://www.upi.com.

Glazer, M. P., and P. M. Glazer. 1989. *The Whistleblowers: Exposing Corruption in Government and Industry.* New York: Basic Books.

Golden, M. M. 1992. "Exit, Voice, Loyalty, and Neglect: Bureaucratic Responses to Presidential Control during the Reagan Administration." *Journal of Public Administration Research and Theory* 2 (1): 29–62.

———. 2000. *What Motivates Bureaucrats? Politics and Administration during the Reagan Years.* New York: Columbia University Press.

Goodsell, C. T. 2004. *The Case for Bureaucracy: A Public Administration Polemic.* 4th ed. Washington, DC: CQ Press.

Gormley, W. T., Jr. 1989. *Taming the Bureaucracy: Muscles, prayers, and Other Strategies.* Princeton, NJ: Princeton University Press.

Gortner, H. F. 2000. "Interview with Al Zuck." Electronic Hallway at the Evans School of Public Affairs, University of Washington, Seattle.

Green, T. 1985. "Regional News." UPI, October 9. http://www.upi.com.

Greenwald, G. 2011. "The Intellectual Cowardice of Bradley Manning's Critics." *Salon,* January 28.

Gummer, B. 1986. "'Committing the Truth': Whistle-Blowing, Organizational Dissent, and the Honorable Bureaucrat." *Administration in Social Work* 9 (4): 89–102.

Halperin, M. 2006. *Bureaucratic Politics and Foreign Policy.* 2nd ed. Washington, DC: Brookings Institution Press.

Halperin, M., and A. Kanter, eds. 1973. *Readings in American Foreign Policy: A Bureaucratic Perspective.* Boston: Little, Brown.

Hansen, E. 2011. "Manning-Lamo Chat Logs Revealed." *Wired,* July 13. http://www .wired.com/threatlevel/2011/07/manning-lamo-logs.

Harris, T. 1991. *Death in the Marsh.* Washington, DC: Island Press.

Heclo, H. 1978. "Issue Networks and the Executive Establishment." In *The New Political System,* ed. A. King, 87–124. Washington, DC: American Enterprise Institute for Public Policy Research.

Hedin, U., and S. Mansson. 2012. "Whistleblowing Processes in Swedish Public Organizations: Complaints and Consequences." *European Journal of Social Work* 15 (2): 151–167.

Heintzman, R. 2007. "Public-Service Values and Ethics: Dead End or Strong Foundation?" *Canadian Public Administration* 50 (4): 573–602.

Hirschman, A. O. 1970. *Exit, Voice, and Loyalty: Responses to Decline in Firms, Organizations, and States.* Cambridge, MA: Harvard University Press.

Hitchner, S. B. 1994. "California Legal Services, Inc." Kennedy School of Government, Harvard University.

Holwager, J. 1976. "Forester Fired in Vehicle Trails Dispute." *Louisville Courier-Journal,* February 11.

Howlett, M. 2011. "Public Managers as the Missing Variable in Policy Studies: An Empirical Investigation Using Canadian Data." *Review of Policy Research* 28 (3): 247–263.

Howlett, M., and R. M. Walker. 2012. "Public Managers in the Policy Process: More Evidence on the Missing Variable?" *Policy Studies Journal* 40 (2): 211–233.

Jaffe, G., and J. Partlow. 2010. "Mullen Says Leak Put Troops and Afghans in Danger; WikiLeaks Documents Include Names of Informants Helping U.S." *Washington Post,* July 30.

Janis, I. 1972. *Victims of Groupthink.* Boston: Houghton Mifflin.

Jasper, C. 2011. "Environmental Degradation on the Hoosier Caused by All Terrain Vehicles." *Hoosier National Forest Highlights,* no. 47, May 10. http://www.fs.usda .gov/Internet/FSE_DOCUMENTS/stelprdb5302778.pdf.

Johnson, R. A. 2003. *Whistleblowing: When It Works—and Why.* Boulder, CO: Lynne Rienner.

Johnson, R. A., and M. E. Kraft. 1990. "Bureaucratic Whistleblowing and Policy Change." *Western Political Quarterly* 43 (4): 849–874.

Jordan, D. 1974. "Suit to Be Filed by Isaac [*sic*] Walton League." *Bedford Daily Times-Mail,* October 16.

———. 1976. "Girton Defends Ferguson Firing: 'Employes [*sic*] Shouldn't Criticize.'" *Bloomington Daily Herald-Telephone,* February 11.

Jos, P. H., M. E. Tompkins, and S. W. Hays. 1989. "In Praise of Difficult People: A Portrait of the Committed Whistleblower." *Public Administration Review* 49 (6): 552–561.

Joseph, G. 1976a. "Forest Service Worker Fired." *Indiana Daily Student,* February 12.

———. 1976b. "Forester Fired: Supervisor Admits to Trail Deviations." *Indiana Daily Student,* February 13.

Kalikow, B. N. 1984. "Environmental Risk: Power to the People." *Technology Review,* October.

Kaptein, M. 2011. "From Inaction to External Whistleblowing: The Influence of the Ethical Culture of Organizations on Employee Responses to Observed Wrongdoing." *Journal of Business Ethics* 98 (3): 513–530.

Katz, D., and R. L. Kahn. 1978. *The Social Psychology of Organizations.* 2nd ed. New York: John Wiley.

Kaufman, H. 1960. *The Forest Ranger.* Baltimore: Johns Hopkins University Press.

Kavanagh, S., and H. E. Ojalvo. 2010. "State's Secrets: Teaching about WikiLeaks." Learning Network: Teaching & Learning with the New York Times, November 30. http://learning.blogs.nytimes.com/2010/11/30/states-secrets-teaching-about-wikileaks.

Keast, R., M. P. Mandell, K. Brown, and G. Woolcock. 2004. "Network Structures: Working Differently and Changing Expectations." *Public Administration Review* 64 (3): 363–371.

Kettl, D. F. 2002. *The Transformation of Governance: Public Administration for Twenty-First Century America.* Baltimore: Johns Hopkins University Press.

———. 2011. *The Politics of the Administrative Process.* 5th ed. Washington, DC: CQ Press.

Key, V. O. 1958. *Politics, Parties, and Pressure Groups.* New York: Thomas Y. Crowell.

Kingdon, J. W. 2010. *Agendas, Alternatives, and Public Policies.* 2nd ed. New York: Pearson.

Kozak, D. C. 1988. *Bureaucratic Politics and National Security: Theory and Practice.* Boulder, CO: Lynne Rienner.

Lame, M. L. 2005. *A Worm in the Teacher's Apple: Protecting America's School Children from Pests and Pesticides.* Bloomington, IN: AuthorHouse.

LaPorte, T. R. 1996. "Shifting Vantage and Conceptual Puzzles in Understanding Public Organization Networks." *Journal of Public Administration Research and Theory* 6 (1): 49–74.

Lash, J., K. Gillman, and D. Sheridan. 1984. *A Season of Spoils: The Reagan Administration's Attack on the Environment.* New York: Pantheon.

Lawrence, P. R., and J. W. Lorsch. 1969. *Developing Organizations: Diagnosis and Action.* Reading, MA: Addison-Wesley.

Lennon, R. 2010. "Case Study of the WikiLeaks Whistleblower." Dublin City University, December 10. http://www.ruairi.info/ethics.pdf.

Levine, H. 1996. *In Search of Sugihara.* New York: Free Press.

Lewis, E. 1980. *Public Entrepreneurship: Toward a Theory of Bureaucratic Political Power.* Bloomington: Indiana University Press.

————. 1988. *American Politics in a Bureaucratic Age: Citizens, Constituents, Clients and Victims.* Lanham, MD: University Press of America.

Lindblom, C. E. 1959. "The Science of 'Muddling Through.'" *Public Administration Review* 19 (2): 79–88.

Lindley, T. 1976. "Forester Embroiled in Controversy." *Evansville Sunday Courier and Press,* February 29.

Lipsky, M. 2010. *Street-Level Bureaucracy: Dilemmas of the Individual in Public Services.* 30th Anniversary expanded ed. New York: Russell Sage.

Long, N. E. 1949. "Power and Administration." *Public Administration Review* 9 (4): 257–264.

Loyens, K., and J. Maesschalck. 2010. "Toward a Theoretical Framework for Ethical Decision Making of Street-Level Bureaucracy: Existing Models Reconsidered." *Administration and Society* 42 (1): 66–100.

Lynn, L. E., Jr. 2012. "Rick Green Has Seen the Enemy: Guess Who?" *Administration and Society* 44 (6): 754–765.

Marmor, T. R. 1990. "Entrepreneurship in Public Management: Wilbur Cohen and Robert Ball." In *Leadership and Innovation: Entrepreneurs in Government,* abridged ed., ed. J. W. Doig and E. C. Hargrove. Baltimore: Johns Hopkins University Press.

Mashaw, J. L. 1985. *Bureaucratic Justice.* New Haven, CT: Yale University Press.

Mason, D. E. 1996. *Leading and Managing the Expressive Dimension: Harnessing the Hidden Power Source of the Nonprofit Sector.* San Francisco: Jossey-Bass.

Maynard-Moody, S., and M. Musheno. 2003. *Cops, Teachers, Counselors: Stories from the Front Lines of Public Service.* Ann Arbor: University of Michigan Press.

Meier, K. J. 1978. "Building Bureaucratic Coalitions." In *The New Politics of Food,* ed. D. F. Hadwiger and W. P. Browne, 57–64. Lexington, MA: Lexington Books.

————. 1988. *The Politics of Insurance.* Albany: State University of New York Press.

————. 1994. *The Politics of Sin: Drugs, Alcohol, and Public Policy.* Armonk, NY: M. E. Sharpe.

Meier, K. J., and J. Bohte. 2006. *Politics and the Bureaucracy: Policymaking in the Fourth Branch of Government.* 5th ed. Belmont, CA: Wadsworth, Cengage Learning.

Meier, K. J., and C. M. Johnson. 1990. "The Politics of Demon Rum: Regulating Alcohol and Its Deleterious Consequences." *American Politics Quarterly* 18 (4): 404–429.

Meier, K. J., and D. R. McFarlane. 1996. "Statutory Coherence and Policy Implementation: The Case of Family Planning." *Journal of Public Policy* 15 (3): 281–298.

Meier, K. J., and D. R. Morgan. 1982. "Citizen Compliance with Public Policy: The National Maximum Speed Law." *Western Political Quarterly* 35 (2): 258–273.

Meier, K. J., and J. Stewart Jr. 1991. *The Politics of Hispanic Education.* Albany: State University of New York Press.

Menzel, D. C. 1999. "Public Managers as Moral Mutes with Ethical Voices: Can They Have It Both Ways?" *PA Times* 22 (8): 4–5.

Miceli, M. P., J. P. Near, M. T. Rehg, and J. R. Van Scotter. 2012. "Predicting Employee Reactions to Perceived Organizational Wrongdoing: Demoralization, Justice, Proactive Personality, and Whistle Blowing." *Human Relations* 65 (8): 923–954.

Milward, H. B. 1980. "Policy Entrepreneurship and Bureaucratic Demand Creation." In *Why Policies Succeed or Fail*, ed. H. M. Ingram and D. E. Mann. Beverly Hills, CA: Sage.

Mintrom, M., and P. Norman. 2009. "Policy Entrepreneurship and Policy Change." *Policy Studies Journal* 37 (4): 649–667.

Moynihan, D. P., and S. K. Pandey. 2008. "The Ties That Bind: Social Networks, Person-Organization Value Fit, and Turnover Intention." *Journal of Public Administration Research and Theory* 18 (2): 205–227.

Mosher, F. 1968. *Democracy and the Public Service.* New York: Oxford University Press.

Nakashima, E. 2011. "Bradley Manning Is at the Center of the WikiLeaks Controversy. But Who Is He?" *Washington Post,* May 4. http://www.washingtonpost.com/lifestyle/magazine/who-is-wikileaks-suspect-bradley-manning/2011/04/16/AFMwBmrF_print.html.

Nappe, T. 1989. "Working Together: Formation of the Lahontan Valley Wetlands Coalition." Paper presented at the Lahontan Audubon Conference, March 24.

National Research Council. 1989. *Irrigation-Induced Water Quality Problems.* Washington, DC: National Academy Press.

Near, J. P., and M. P. Miceli. 1986. "Retaliation against Whistle Blowers: Predictors and Effects." *Journal of Applied Psychology* 71 (1): 137–145.

Needleman, M. L., and C. E. Needleman. 1974. *Guerrillas in the Bureaucracy: The Community Planning Experiment in the United States.* New York: John Wiley.

Neustadt, R. E., and E. May. 1986. *Thinking in Time: The Uses of History for Decision Makers.* New York: Free Press.

Nicks, D. 2012. *Private: Bradley Manning, WikiLeaks, and the Biggest Exposure of Official Secrets in American History.* Chicago: Chicago Review Press.

Oberfield, Z. W. 2010. "Rule Following and Discretion at Government's Frontlines: Continuity and Change during Organization Socialization." *Journal of Public Administration Research and Theory* 20 (4): 735–755.

———. 2012. "Socialization and Self-Selection: How Police Officers Develop Their Views about Using Force." *Administration and Society* 44 (6): 702–730.

O'Connor, J. D. 2005. "I'm the Guy They Called Deep Throat." *Vanity Fair,* July, 86–89, 129–133.

O'Kelly, C., and M. Dubnick. 2006. "Taking Tough Choices Seriously: Public Administration and Individual Moral Agency." *Journal of Public Administration Research and Theory* 16 (3): 393–415.

O'Leary, R. 1994. "The Bureaucratic Politics Paradox: The Case of Wetlands Legislation in Nevada." *Journal of Public Administration Research and Theory* 4 (4): 443–467.

O'Leary, R., and L. Bingham. 2007. *A Manager's Guide to Resolving Conflicts in Collaborative Networks.* Washington, DC: IBM Center for the Business of Government.

———, eds. 2009. *The Collaborative Public Manager.* Washington, DC: Georgetown University Press.

O'Leary, R., Y. Choi, and C. Gerard. 2012. "The Skill Set of the Successful Collaborator." *Public Administration Review* 72 (S1): 70–83.

O'Leary, R., R. F. Durant, D. J. Fiorino, and P. S. Weiland. 1999. *Managing for the Environment: Understanding the Legal, Organizational, and Policy Challenges.* San Francisco: Jossey-Bass.

O'Leary, R., and C. Gerard. 2012. *Collaboration across Boundaries: Insights and Tips from Federal Senior Executives.* Washington, DC: IBM Center for the Business of Government.

———. 2013. "Collaborative Governance and Leadership: A 2012 Survey of Local Government Collaboration." In *The Municipal Yearbook,* 43–56. Washington, DC: International City/County Management Association.

O'Leary, R., and N. Vij. 2012. "Collaborative Public Management: Where Have We Been and Where Are We Going?" *American Review of Public Administration* 42 (5): 507–522.

O'Toole, L. J. 1997. "Treating Networks Seriously: Practical and Research-Based Agendas in Public Administration." *Public Administration Review* 57 (1): 45–52.

Park, H., and J. Blenkinsopp. 2009. "Whistleblowing as Planned Behavior: A Survey of South Korean Police Officers." *Journal of Business Ethics* 85 (4): 545–556.

Perry, J. L., A. Hondeghem, and L. R. Wise. 2010. "Revisiting the Motivational Bases of Public Service: Twenty Years of Research and an Agenda for the Future." *Public Administration Review* 70 (5): 681–690.

Peters, B. G. 2009. *The Politics of Bureaucracy.* 6th ed. New York: Longman.

Poulsen, K., and K. Zetter. 2010. "U.S. Intelligence Analyst Arrested in WikiLeaks Video Probe." *Wired,* June 6. http://www.wired.com/threatlevel/2010/06/leak.

Provan, K. G., and J. B. Milward. 1995. "A Preliminary Theory of Interorganizational Network Effectiveness: A Comparative Study of Four Community Mental Health Systems." *Administrative Science Quarterly* 40 (1): 1–33.

Punch, M. 1984. "The Divided Organization: Deviance, Conflict and Defense in Police Work." *Police Studies* 7 (1): 3–18.

Rhodes, R. A. W., and D. Marsh. 1992. "New Directions in the Study of Policy Networks." *European Journal of Political Research* 21 (2): 181–205.

Riccucci, N. M. 1995. *Unsung Heroes: Federal Execucrats Making a Difference.* Washington, DC: Georgetown University Press.

———. 2005. "Street-Level Bureaucrats and Intrastate Variation in the Implementation of Temporary Assistance for Needy Families Policy." *Journal of Public Administration Research and Theory* 15 (1): 89–111.

Richardson, W. D. 1997. *Democracy, Bureaucracy, and Character: Founding Thought.* Lawrence: University Press of Kansas.

Ridout, C. F. 1974. "Job Corps." Harvard Business School, Harvard University.

Ripley, R. B., and G. A. Franklin. 1991. *Congress, the Bureaucracy, and Public Policy.* 5th ed. Pacific Grove, CA: Brooks/Cole.

Roberts, N. C., and P. J. King. 1987. "Policy Entrepreneurs: Catalysts for Policy Innovation." *Journal of State Government* 60 (4): 172–178.

———. 1991. "Policy Entrepreneurs: Their Activity Structure and Function in the Policy Process." *Journal of Public Administration Research and Theory* 1 (2): 147–175.

———. 1996. *Transforming Public Policy.* San Francisco: Jossey-Bass.

Rohr, J. A. 1986. *To Run a Constitution: The Legitimacy of the Administrative State.* Lawrence: University Press of Kansas.

———. 1989. *Ethics for Bureaucrats: An Essay on Law and Values.* 2nd ed. New York: Marcel Dekker.

Rosenbloom, D. H., J. D. Carroll, and J. D. Carroll. 2000. *Constitutional Competence for Public Managers: Cases and Commentary.* Itasca, IL: F. E. Peacock.

Rothwell, G. R., and J. N. Baldwin. 2007. "Whistle-Blowing and the Code of Silence in Police Agencies." *Crime & Delinquency* 53 (4): 605–632.

Rourke, F. E. 1984. *Bureaucracy, Politics, and Public Policy.* 3rd ed. New York: Addison-Wesley.

Rusbridger, A. 2011. "WikiLeaks: The Guardian's Role in the Biggest Leak in the History of the World." *Guardian,* January 28.

Rusbult, C. E., D. Farrell, G. Rogers, and A. G. Mainous III. 1988. "Impact of Exchange Variables on Exit, Voice, Loyalty, and Neglect: An Integrative Model of Responses to Declining Job Satisfaction." *Academy of Management Journal* 31 (3): 599–627.

Rusco, E. 1992. "The Truckee-Carson-Pyramid Lake Water Rights Settlement Act and Pyramid Lake." *Nevada Public Affairs Review* 1: 9–14.

Savage, C. 2012. "WikiLeaks Case Lawyer Chides Marine Jailers on Manning's Treatment." *New York Times,* December 11.

———. 2013. "Soldier Admits Providing Files to WikiLeaks." *New York Times,* February 28. http://www.nytimes.com/2013/03/01/us/bradley-manning-admits-giving-trove-of-military-data-to-wikileaks.html?pagewanted=all&_r=0.

Seidman, H. 1998. *Politics, Position, and Power: The Dynamics of Federal Organization.* 5th ed. New York: Oxford University Press.

Selznick, P. 2011. *TVA and the Grass Roots.* 2nd ed. New York: Quid Pro LLC.

Ser, S. 2012. "Did a WikiLeaks Document Doom a 'Mossad Agent'?" *Times of Israel,* May 16.

Shane, S. 2011. "Accused Soldier in Brig as WikiLeaks Link Is Sought." *New York Times,* January 13.

Shanker, T. 2010. "Loophole May Have Aided Theft of Classified Data." *New York Times,* July 8.

Shaughnessy, M. F. 1981. "Social Control and Organization Deviance." *Quarterly Journal of Ideology* 5 (2): 26–33.

Sims, R. L. 2009. "A Study of Deviance as a Retaliatory Response to Organizational Power." *Journal of Business Ethics* 92 (4): 553–563.

Slaikeu, K. A., and R. H. Hasson. 1998. *Controlling the Costs of Conflict: How to Design a System for Your Organization.* San Francisco: Jossey-Bass.

Slater, P., and W. Bennis. 1990. "Democracy Is Inevitable." *Harvard Business Review* 68 (5): 167–177.

Snapp, R. 1976. "Ferguson Fired by U.S. Forest Service." *Bedford Daily Times-Mail,* February 10.

———. 1977a. "Attorney Has No Comment in ORV Policy Case." *Bedford Daily Times-Mail,* October 19.

———. 1977b. "Forest Service Withdraws Off-Road-Vehicle Policy." *Bedford Daily Times-Mail,* October 28.

———. 1977c. "Forester Applauds ORV Policy Withdrawal; Says Questions Still Unanswered in His Case." *Bedford Daily Times-Mail,* November 5.

Society of Professionals in Dispute Resolution. 2001. "Report: Characteristics of Integrated Conflict Management Systems." SPIDR, Washington, DC.

Stanfield, R. L. 1985. "Enough and Clean Enough?" *National Journal,* August 17.

Stein, H. 1952. *Public Administration and Policy Development.* New York: Harcourt, Brace and World.

Stillman, R., II. 2004. *The American Bureaucracy: The Core of Modern Government.* 3rd ed. Belmont, CA: Wadsworth, Cengage Learning.

Strickland, R. 1992. "Stillwater: Its Friends and Neighbors." *Nevada Public Affairs Review* 1: 68–73.

Sullivan, P. 2005. "CIA Agent Gust L. Avrakotos Dies at Age 67." *Washington Post,* December 25.

Thompson, J. D. 1967. *Organizations in Action.* New York: McGraw-Hill.

Timm, T., and R. Reitman. 2013. "Freedom of the Press Foundation Publishes Leaked Audio of Bradley Manning's Statement." Freedom of the Press Foundation, March 11. https://pressfreedomfoundation.org/blog/2013/03/fpf-publishes-leaked-audio-of-bradley-mannings-statement.

Ting, M. M. 2008. "Whistleblowing." *American Political Science Review* 102 (2): 249–267.

Truelson, J. A. 1985. "Protest Is Not a Four Letter Word." *Bureaucrat,* Summer.

Tummers, L. G., and S. Van de Walle. 2012. "Explaining Health Care Professionals' Resistance to Implement Diagnosis Related Groups: (No) Benefits for Society, Patients and Professionals." *Health Policy* 108 (2–3): 158–166.

Turner, W. 1984. "Puget Sound Cities Ordered to Clean Up Sewage." *New York Times,* October 1.

Tyler, T. R., P. E. Callahan, and J. Frost. 2007. "Armed and Dangerous(?): Motivating Rule Adherence among Agents of Social Control." *Law and Society Review* 41 (2): 457–492.

Ury, W. L., J. M. Brett, and S. B. Goldberg. 1993. *Getting Disputes Resolved: Designing Systems to Cut the Costs of Conflict.* San Francisco: Jossey-Bass.

U.S. Department of Agriculture, Office of Investigation. 1975. Investigation report. June 5.

U.S. Department of the Interior. 1989. *The Impact of Federal Programs on Wetlands.* Washington, DC: Government Printing Office.

U.S. Environmental Protection Agency. 1983. *Investigation of John Spencer, Regional Administrator.* Inspector General Report. Washington, DC: Government Printing Office, August 8.

———. 1988. *Investigation of Robie Russell, Regional Administrator.* Inspector General Report. Washington, DC: Government Printing Office, July 5.

———. 1990a. *Investigation of Robie Russell, Regional Administrator.* Inspector General Report. Washington, DC: Government Printing Office, January 31.

———. 1990b. *Investigation of Robie Russell, Regional Administrator.* Inspector General Report. Washington, DC: Government Printing Office, February 26.

Uys, T. 2008. "Rational Loyalty and Whistleblowing: The South African Context." *Current Sociology* 56 (6): 904–921.

Vadera, A. K., R. V. Aguilera, and B. B. Caza. 2009. "Making Sense of Whistle-Blowing's Antecedents: Learning from Research on Identity and Ethics Programs." *Business Ethics Quarterly* 19 (4): 553–586.

Vandekerckhove, W., and E. E. Tsahuridu. 2010. "Risky Rescues and the Duty to Blow the Whistle." *Journal of Business Ethics* 97 (3): 365–380.

Van Wart, M. 1996. "The Sources of Ethical Decision Making for Individuals in the Public Sector." *Public Administration Review* 56 (6): 525–533.

Vinzant, J. C., and L. Crothers. 1998. *Street-Level Leadership: Discretion and Legitimacy in Front-Line Public Service.* Washington, DC: Georgetown University Press.

Waldo, D. 1988. *The Enterprise of Public Administration: A Summary View.* Novato, CA: Chandler and Sharp.

West, W. F. 1985. *Administrative Rulemaking: Politics and Processes.* Westport, CT: Greenwood Press.

———. 1995. *Controlling the Bureaucracy: Institutional Constraints in Theory and Practice.* Armonk, NY: M. E. Sharpe.

Wildavsky, A. 1986. *Budgeting.* 2nd ed. New Brunswick, NJ: Transaction.

———. 2000. *The Politics of the Budgetary Process.* 4th ed. New York: Scott Foresman.

———. 2004. *Leadership in a Small Town.* 2nd ed. New Brunswick, NJ: Transaction.

Wilson, D. 1990. "Reception Food Order Called into Question—Cost Hidden in Rent, EPA Employee Says." *Seattle Times,* February 19.

Witesman, E. M., and C. R. Wise. 2012. "The Reformer's Spirit: How Public Administrators Fuel Training in the Skills of Good Governance." *Public Administration Review* 72 (5): 710–720.

Wood, B. D., and R. Waterman. 1991. "The Dynamics of Political Control of the Bureaucracy." *American Political Science Review* 85 (3): 801–828.

———. 1994. *Bureaucratic Dynamics: The Role of Bureaucracy in a Democracy.* Boulder, CO: Westview Press.

Woutat, Donald. 1987. "Caribou Refuge: Wildlife or Oil? Debate Stirs Alaska." *Los Angeles Times,* August 19.

Young, J. 1976. "Ferguson Firing." *Bedford Daily-Times Mail,* February 12.

Index